KILLING THE WITTIGO

INDIGENOUS CULTURE-BASED APPROACHES TO WAKING UP, TAKING ACTION, AND DOING THE WORK OF HEALING

A Book for Young Adults

By Suzanne Methot

LIBRARY AND ARCHIVES CANADA CATALOGUING IN
PUBLICATION

Title: Killing the Wittigo : Indigenous culture-
based approaches to waking up, taking action,
and doing the work of healing : a book for young
adults / by Suzanne Methot.

Names: Methot, Suzanne, 1968- author. |
Adaptation of (work): Methot, Suzanne, 1968-
Legacy.

Identifiers: Canadiana (print) 20230164803 |
Canadiana (ebook) 20230165753

ISBN 978-1-77041-724-3 (softcover)
ISBN 978-1-77852-153-9 (ePub)
ISBN 978-1-77852-154-6 (PDF)
ISBN 978-1-77852-155-3 (Kindle)

Subjects: LCSH: Indigenous peoples—
Canada—Social conditions. | LCSH: Indigenous
peoples—Health and hygiene—Canada. | LCSH:
Colonization—Social aspects—Canada. | LCSH:
Colonization—Psychological aspects. | LCSH:
Psychic trauma—Canada.

Classification: LCC RA448.5.I5 M47 2023 | DDC
362.1089/97071—dc23

Published by ECW Press
665 Gerrard Street East
Toronto, Ontario, Canada M4M 1Y2
416-694-3348 / info@ecwpress.com

Editor for the Press: Susan Renouf
Cover Design and Typesetting: Jessica Albert
Wittigo Illustration: Mapris Purgas

This book is funded in part by the Government of Canada. *Ce livre est financé en partie par le gouvernement du Canada.* We acknowledge the support of the Canada Council for the Arts. *Nous remercions le Conseil des arts du Canada de son soutien.* We acknowledge the funding support of the Ontario Arts Council (OAC), an agency of the Government of Ontario. We also acknowledge the support of the Government of Ontario through the Ontario Book Publishing Tax Credit, and through Ontario Creates.

ONTARIO ARTS COUNCIL
CONSEIL DES ARTS DE L'ONTARIO
an Ontario government agency
un organisme du gouvernement de l'Ontario

Canada Council   Conseil des arts
for the Arts   du Canada

Canadä

PRINTED AND BOUND IN CANADA

PRINTING: MARQUIS   5   4   3   2   1

CONTENTS

DISCLAIMER

A note to you, the amazing person who has picked up this book: I am a trained educator and agency worker by profession and a helper by clan/spirit name, but it's impossible for me to enter into a helper-client relationship with all of my readers. The information inside this book is accurate, but what's here is not a substitute for getting care or treatment from a recognized elder, medicine person, support worker, counsellor/therapist, teacher, or health-care professional who can respond to your unique needs and specific circumstances.

WELCOME

Hi there. Thanks for being brave and picking up this book. I wrote it for you and for all the people you know.

This book explains how colonization has led to trauma in Indigenous peoples, families, and communities. It explains how trauma gets passed down in families through generations and the effect that this cycle of intergenerational trauma has on our everyday lives and relationships. It also shares stories about the healing work that is being done in urban, rural, and reserve/reservation communities across the Americas. It includes the words of young people who have started their own journeys of decolonization, healing, and change.

I wrote this book to help you understand your life, your family, and your community a little bit better. I want this book to take you beyond survival, beyond resilience, toward well-being and achieving your goals. This is the book I wish I'd had when I was younger.

Part of what this book does is help you live in the present day. Trauma keeps us locked in the past — trapped in unresolved emotions, too many memories (this is known as hypervigilance, and it's in the book), not enough memories (dissociation, also in the book), and always feeling unsafe. Carrying around all this stuff is hard. It creates a lot of anger, shame, and self-blame. It stops you from living the life you want. I wrote this book to help you let go of that burden, so you can be the person you were born to be.

If you're a young person who has survived trauma, this book will help you love yourself more. If you're a parent, it will help you see the cycles you're a part of and may be passing down. If you're a cop, a doctor, or you work in a dominant society system or institution, it will help you understand the links between settler colonialism, systemic racism, and contemporary challenges in Indigenous communities. If you're a teacher, social worker, or other helper, it will show you effective ways to reach kids who are in distress. This book is for everyone, Indigenous and non-Indigenous.

There are lots of happy stories in Indigenous communities and amazing projects going on every single day. I've included some of those stories in this book. But this book focuses on the hard stuff: the things we're ashamed to talk about, the things we don't understand but want to figure out, the things we see and want to change, and all the wrong ideas we have about ourselves. The fact that we've survived colonization shows how awesome Indigenous peoples are.

But underneath all that awesomeness is a deep sense of terror, anger, grief, and loss. There is still so much work we need to do to resist and counteract the effects of colonization.

Change happens in different ways for different people. This book is intended as a resource you can grow into. You can read a bit and then stop for a while if it gets to be too much. You can throw it across the room when it pisses you off, then pick it up again later when you're ready. The information in this book is organized in chunks, so you can open any page and engage with whatever is there. Then, if that's all you can handle on that day, no problem. You can put the book down again and open it up to another random page on another random day.

This book is trauma informed. That means that I try to keep you safe while you read it. Being safe relates to having choices. Before we talk about terrible things, there's a description of what's coming up. Then I tell you how we're going to support you in dealing with that information, and I ask you if you would like to turn the page. At all times, you have a choice and give your consent. I've also included a Flashback Protocol before the first section, so you have something to do/ use if you're feeling overwhelmed at any point. The book opens and closes with an invocation, so you can call in your spirit helpers at the start and end of every time you read.

Some Indigenous people still aren't ready to talk about intergenerational trauma. They think talking about trauma pulls focus away from colonialism in the Americas. They think we should only tell positive stories about the good work being done in Indigenous communities. But the good things are only part of the story. If we want healing, we need to get real. Acknowledging the negative effects that colonization has on our families and communities is a crucial step toward change.

But it's not just about looking inward. The systems and institutions of the dominant society are not trauma or healing informed, and they almost always punish young people for engaging in trauma-related behaviours. I wrote this book so that you have the information you need to better understand those systems and institutions, and to give you some ideas about how you can advocate for yourself within them.

Too often, we see young leaders step away from decolonization and cultural reclamation work in order to deal with their own mental, physical, and spiritual health. I want this book to offer young change-makers the support you need to continue your work.

Indigenous youth are the fastest growing population in the Americas. You are the future — and someday you will also be ancestors. What kind of world do we want to live in? What do we want to leave behind for the next 7 generations? To plan it, we have to tell stories that explain how we got here. To create it, we have to draw a roadmap for personal and collective change. To live it, we have to hold tight to a transformative vision for the future, one that revitalizes and prioritizes Indigenous culture-based approaches.

There's a list of adverse childhood experiences (also called ACEs) in this book. So here's something you should know: I have experienced every single one of the items on that list. Reading it changed my life. Suddenly, I wasn't the only one. The things that I'd experienced, that seemed shameful or unmentionable, were there in plain sight. That list forced me to admit things I had never spoken out loud, even to myself, in my own head and heart.

Healing from intergenerational trauma is about revealing the real you. Sometimes that means getting down to the hard stuff that's in this book. But that hard stuff isn't all I am, and it isn't all you are. The other stories you carry — the stories of strength, love, joy, and resistance — are waiting to be discovered, too.

You are worthy of love. You are capable of change. Even if you've done harm, you still deserve support.

Life is good when you really start living it.

FLASHBACK PROTOCOL

If you ever feel overwhelmed, fearful, or like the world around you has disappeared and you're in another place, you can use the Flashback Protocol to ground yourself before you continue reading.

Right now I am feeling _____
(scared, anxious, panicky, sad . . .)

I am sensing in my body _____
(heart racing, stomach tightening, shaking, sweating, dizzy, headache, nausea . . .)

Because I am remembering _____
(bad things, the bad person, that awful stuff . . .)

It is now _____
(name the time, date, year . . . if you need to, look at a clock or check your phone)

And I am here at _____
(name the place)

And I can see _____
(name 5 objects you can see around you)

So I know that _____
is not happening now

INVOCATION

In this space, we are centering healing.

Think of all the ancestors, those whose names you know and those whose names you don't know, who have brought you into your existence.

Invite them into this space with you now.

1

TERROR, ANGER, GRIEF, LOSS

Indigenous peoples are more than victims, and the story of colonization is not the only story we tell. But what we inherit from colonialism creates a circular reliving of the trauma, generation after generation.

TERROR

Your children are taken away by police to a boarding/residential school, 1954.

A police car slows down beside you as you walk on the sidewalk, 2018.

ANGER

Settlers in your territory build cabins on your family's trapline, 1972.

The colonial government goes ahead with a dam project that will flood treaty land, 2021.

GRIEF

The US Army shoots millions of bison and uses the bones to make sugar, fertilizer, and dinner plates, 1870.

You see a photo of bison skulls piled up at a railway yard, waiting to be shipped to England, 2015.

LOSS

The colonial government puts harvesting restrictions on your nation and locks people up for gathering medicines in a park, 1937.

An Indigenous knowledge keeper dies of diabetes, 2022.

These things happen/ed to real people. For Indigenous people, the past is not the past — it's today, right now.

Trauma keeps you in a loop with your past. If you experience/d trauma in childhood, you might be 15 years old, or 25 years old, but sometimes still think and act like you're 8 years old.

That's why you please other people and don't respect your own boundaries. That's why you work too much and ignore your own needs. That's why you never ask for help. That's why you stay in unhealthy relationships. You're behaving like your wounded childhood self, acting out the feelings created by the trauma and using coping strategies you learned at that time.

Trauma is a response to a terrible event (or series of events). It affects mind, body, spirit, and emotion. But there's nothing wrong with you. You just have to unlearn your survival patterns and learn how to be different.

COLONIZATION SUCKS!
YOU DON'T.

WHY INDIGENOUS PEOPLE CAN'T JUST "GET OVER IT"

Europeans began colonizing the Americas in the 1400s. They came for gold, furs, wood, and crops including corn, cotton, and tobacco. Millions of Indigenous people were killed by enslavement, genocide, and disease.

Sometimes, Indigenous people and settlers lived peacefully and exchanged ideas. But settlers wanted to make money, which meant they had to control the land. Indigenous peoples were pushed to the margins of society, and Indigenous economic systems, governance systems, and social structures were damaged or destroyed.

Today, Indigenous people continue to succeed despite colonization, becoming nurses, artists, teachers, and engineers. But Indigenous people also experience high rates of poverty and poor health, barriers in education, and the everyday impacts of intergenerational trauma.

HISTORIC TRAUMA

- murder and genocide
- disease (smallpox, tuberculosis)
- treaty promises not honoured (medicine, farming tools)
- imprisonment of spiritual/political leaders
- bison extirpated from the Americas by colonial governments who wanted to starve Indigenous peoples off the land
- Indigenous peoples relocated to unknown territories in order to establish settler society and colonial sovereignty
- Indigenous people confined to reserves/reservations (some reserves less than 10% of traditional territory) and forbidden from leaving without permission
- Indigenous communities purposely allocated land of poor agricultural quality
- Indian Act creates government-controlled system of identity/

belonging; federal government assumes control over everyday life for status Indians (Canada)
- Dawes Act creates government-controlled system of identity/
belonging; makes communal land into private land; 90
million acres of land stripped from Indigenous nations (US)
- colonial/patriarchal governance systems forced upon
Indigenous communities
- re-education in residential/boarding/day schools (separation
from family, siblings, community; punished for speaking
Indigenous languages; psychological, emotional, physical,
sexual abuse; religious indoctrination; hard labour)
- ceremonies banned

IMPACTS ON 1ST GENERATION

- loss of control over everyday life
- removal/destruction of resources to support healthy living
- negative effect on feelings of safety
- socioeconomic dependence
- struggles with cultural identity
- self-hatred
- disconnection from natural world
- spiritual confusion

INTERGENERATIONAL IMPACTS

- parenting issues (neglect, abuse, shaming)
- rage and anger (toward white people and toward Indigenous
people who speak out or challenge the status quo)
- layers of unresolved grief and loss
- depression
- flashbacks (stuck in past), anxiety (worrying about future)
- self-medicating pain through substance use
- bullying and abusing others after suffering abuse to self
- toxic communication patterns (gossip, put-downs, personal
attacks, secrets)

- disunity/conflict among individuals, families, and factions in the community
- dysfunctional community patterns (malicious talk, organizing/participating in mobs, not supporting/standing with victims)
- re-enacting childhood feelings/behaviours in adult relationships
- low self-esteem (feeling inferior/lesser than other people, especially white people in authority; having no confidence in your abilities; feeling unworthy or that you don't deserve good things; lack of self-respect and inability to set boundaries with others)
- patterns of sexual abuse in families and communities
- feelings of shame, guilt, self-blame
- community leaders who misuse power and authority to control others
- problems with digestion
- problems with sleep
- chronic physical illness related to spiritual and emotional states
- physical abuse
- property crime (wrecking what other people have)
- suicide, thoughts of suicide, threats of suicide
- fear of failure, self-sabotage
- difficulty learning due to emotional states
- not liking things that are "too much like school"
- fear of personal growth, transformation, healing
- voicelessness (feeling like you can't speak your truth)
- feeling powerless . . . like you can't change your life or shape the world around you

COLONIALISM CONTINUES

- racism, discrimination, marginalization (e.g., Indigenous people followed in stores while shopping)

- healthcare system ignores/blames/re-traumatizes Indigenous patients
- resource/extraction projects on unceded and treaty territories (hydroelectric dams, oil sands, fracking, pipelines)
- resource/extraction projects damage/destroy Indigenous food sovereignty (e.g., Line 3 pipeline going through wild rice lakes)
- Indigenous people attacked by settlers for engaging in treaty right to fish/hunt/gather (e.g., fishing conflict between Sipekne'katik First Nation and non-Indigenous lobster fishers)
- Indigenous people arrested for engaging in public protest
- Indigenous activists spied on by government and police
- child welfare system separates families instead of offering supports
- trafficking of Indigenous women and children
- Indigenous people more likely to be killed by police than white people and Black people
- Indigenous people incarcerated at greater rate than non-Indigenous people; longer sentences for Indigenous offenders
- education system does not offer Indigenized or land-based curricula

Forget what you've heard. Indigenous people are NOT flawed, deficient, lesser, or uncivilized! Indigenous people are intelligent, creative, and adaptable.

The unhealthy coping skills you've used — the things you may even be ashamed of — have helped you survive genocide and oppression. There's no shame in survival.

You are a survivor. Love yourself for that.

WHY US

I look around and it hurts
It's taking over my soul
It seems wherever I turn
Our lives are losing control

There's questions plaguing my mind
I look for more than you know
I'm here and I am alive
I feel I'm ready to go

My life isn't pleasant, struck down from the struggle
I'm motivated but our history has me troubled
Knowledge is losing its meaning, we half listen
There is spirit in the land and we have the clan system

The truth blows wind through the trees like cold whistles
This dark cloud hangs over us like smoke signals
Heartbeat of a leader, I'm an Indian with warrior thought
Trust and loyalty is all that we got

They took our land but not traditions and culture
Why us
There is a struggle but it's making us stronger
Why us
Do you see who we are? There's spirit in our hearts
The future seems so far but our time is now
We sing why us

The pain is real, I won't lie
It's hard to see through the fear
It's in my grandparents' eyes
They knew we would be here

I hope that we'll overcome
Let's all go back to the land
There's so much more to be done
We can carry our clan

By Tianna Joseph, Jaydeen Felix, Tre Felix, Landon Joseph-Millard, Devaun Anatole, Scott Hanson, Jenna Felix, Matthew Monk, Keeley Tom, and Mariah Aslin

Youth from Tl'azt'en First Nation (Tachie, British Columbia)

Street medicine, overdosing from the unknown
Sunny side streets, this is where I'm from
Contemplated death and I could say I've come close
We need to listen to the teachings that the elders once told

I thought I'd never break, but I'm sweeping up the pieces
I wanna make my dad proud, and that keeps me dreaming
I'm scared of tomorrow but every day's a baby step
Smudge for the bright future that we pray to get

They took our land but not traditions and culture
Why us
There is a struggle but it's making us stronger
Why us
Do you see who we are? There's spirit in our hearts
The future seems so far but our time is now
We sing why us

I'm motivated and I know I could be going places
I got these fears I'm facing, but I hope you hear me say this
Let's change the way we live our lives on a daily basis
Follow my footsteps, I'm finding hope and I'm leaving traces

I wanna be an inspiration for this generation
Faced with the missing and murdered women, it's devastating
I wanna see my people prosper with no explanations
It's gonna be a challenge, to quiet the frustrations

Take your money, we don't care about the compensation
Our elders been saying that our land is the education
We've decided to bring the hope to this reservation
This is the moment, let's come together as a nation

INDIGENOUS FAMILIES HAVE BEEN RIPPED APART BY COLONIZATION.

When children were taken away to boarding/day/residential schools, elders couldn't pass on knowledge. Generations of Indigenous people did not learn how to love themselves or how to be parents to their children. Children felt like their parents didn't want them or care about them, and often decided not to care for their parents in return. When children returned to their home communities, they didn't fit in, and were often treated as outsiders.

When children are taken into foster care today, they are most often separated from their cultures and traditions. These deliberate government policies were/are aimed at destabilizing Indigenous communities.

Instead of having families broken apart, Indigenous survivors of the foster care system want families to be supported in healing from colonization and intergenerational trauma. Some survivors have started volunteer-run groups that help families navigate the system. The groups also work to keep families together. Other survivors have started peer support groups for young people in/from the foster care system.

"I didn't even know I was Indigenous until I was in my 20s. I didn't know my family was alive. I didn't even know I had siblings. I remember my guidance counsellor telling me that people like me don't get happy endings. People like me don't become lawyers. Those aren't options for foster kids like me. It was a lot of having to parent myself and tell myself that I could do it. . . . There's so many years of lost time that we had, so it's been a healing journey for us. The group is starting to give me that peace and that sense of connection I've longed for."

NATASHA REIMER-OKEMOW
(Cree/Jamaican), Founder, Foster Up

TRIGGER WARNING

This next part might be hard.

We're going to talk about different kinds of abuse, how that abuse makes us feel, and how it changes who and how we are in the world.

You might want to read this next part with someone who can support you. It should be someone you feel safe with.

At the end of this section, there are rituals, checklists, and an activity that will help you stay grounded.

You've already invited your ancestors in. They are with you. Will you turn the page?

**Sexual abuse • Physical abuse
Emotional abuse • Witnessing violence • Not
getting tenderness or caring from parents**

When you experience trauma, your body responds with stress hormones so you can be ready for future traumatic events. Waiting for the next bad thing to happen is an exhausting way to live. Some survivors drink alcohol or use street drugs to help them manage the anger or sadness that they feel, or to help them forget.

When you feel on guard and unsafe all the time, it makes it hard to connect with other people.

NOT ALL CONNECTION IS THE SAME.

If you experience/d trauma in childhood, you might be looking for someone to rescue you or take away your pain. This can put you in dangerous situations, where you hook up with or hang around people who don't really care for you, but who see your need and use it to harm you or gain control over you.

But it's complicated — more than just "victim" and "perpetrator."

This cycle can happen over generations. Indigenous people who harm other Indigenous people were often victimized as children, too.

WE REPEAT WHAT WE DON'T REPAIR.

After you experience trauma, you might start to think differently about yourself and your place in the world. This way of thinking can be passed down in families, as children learn about the world from parents and caregivers who have experienced trauma themselves. It can even be passed from person to person inside communities.

"THE WORLD IS UNSAFE"
"NO ONE WILL HELP ME"
"DON'T TRUST ANYONE"
"I AM NOT WORTHY OF LOVE OR RESPECT"

When you experience trauma, your mind tries to protect you by forgetting. Then the wittigo moves into that space and infects your spirit. To heal that spirit wound, you have to see the wittigo — face it and confront it — and take back that space. Then you really start living your life.

The wittigo is a cannibal spirit creature from the oral traditions of many Indigenous nations. A wittigo can take possession of a person's soul, and it can also haunt a community. When a person is possessed by the wittigo, they lose their humanity, destroying their family members and those they love the most. Stories about the wittigo warn us to practise kindness, sharing, and self-control.

Do you blame yourself when relationships, jobs, school, and living arrangements don't work out? Do you blame yourself for what happened to you?

"IF I'D FOUGHT BACK, MAYBE IT WOULDN'T HAVE HAPPENED"

"I MUST HAVE DONE SOMETHING TO MAKE IT HAPPEN"

When something traumatic happens to us, our boundaries are invaded. We lose our independence and our right to exist or act separately from other people. We also lose control, which means we lose choice. It makes us feel helpless. We start to doubt ourselves, and we no longer trust our own judgment.

The wittigo likes to infect us with shame and self-blame. Shame and self-blame are the stories your abuser wants you to believe.

YOU ARE NOT RESPONSIBLE FOR WHAT HAPPENED TO YOU.

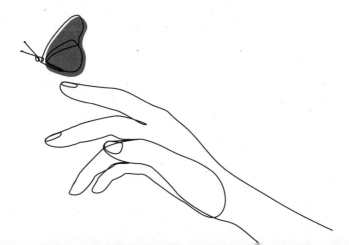

When something is "unresolved," it means it still needs an answer, a solution, an ending. Many Indigenous people have unresolved emotions relating to family experiences and other trauma. The terror, anger, fear, and grief created by the trauma of colonization takes up a lot of space inside our bodies, minds, and spirits.

Maria Yellow Horse Brave Heart (Lakota), says it's hard for Indigenous people to be joyful, free, and happy. Maria says that many Indigenous people create suffering in their lives as a way to mourn their ancestors and keep murdered and missing people alive in their hearts and minds. It's a form of loyalty and remembrance. But these unresolved stories, and the feelings and emotions that go with them, can destroy the survivor's own spirit and have negative effects on their lives.

Is there a way you can mourn your ancestors, remember what has happened during colonization, and still live a joyful life?

RITUALS HELP US CONNECT TO SOMETHING LARGER THAN OURSELVES SO THAT WE DON'T FEEL SO ALONE.

We engage in rituals to seek peace, clear mind/spirit, and gain connection to the land. Rituals connect us to family, culture, society, traditions, ancestors, and ourselves. Sometimes rituals help us let go of things. Rituals don't have to happen on a schedule. They can be daily, weekly, or just happen when they happen. They can be big or small.

- light a candle at a certain time of the day/week for a person who has died, or who you have lost
- create a calming music mix and listen to it right before you go to sleep
- write down bad memories, then bury the paper or throw it in a fire
- carry something special in your pocket to remind you of something or someone, and take it out and hold it when you feel angry, sad, or afraid
- create a work of art with the title "This Is Me" and put it up on your wall
- prepare and eat a special meal in honour of your ancestors (you can do this even if you don't know who your ancestors are)
- sit quietly and watch the sunrise/sunset
- go somewhere alone and yell, scream, or cry as much as you need to

- keep a special pillow that you can hit, punch, or throw when you feel angry
- lie on your back on the floor, put your arms up straight (next to your head), and stretch until you feel better
- take a bath in some wild rose petals or cedar leaves, and tell yourself "I am free to feel" and "I am a sacred part of creation"
- when you feel upset, draw a picture that represents the emotion — let the paper have it so you don't have to carry it anymore

Imagine your anger, grief, and fear as a ball in your chest. Thank it for holding all the pain and negative energy for you. Then imagine that ball leaving your body and taking the pain away with it.

People who experience a greater number of negative events during childhood have a higher risk for later health problems, including headaches, depression, diabetes, and obesity.

ACE stands for adverse childhood experiences. You can calculate your ACE score by answering Yes or No to the following questions.

Before you were 18 years old . . .

Did a parent or other adult in the household often or very often:

> Swear at you, insult you, put you down, or humiliate you?

> Act in a way that made you afraid that you might be physically hurt?

Did a parent or other adult in the household often or very often:

> Push, grab, slap, or throw something at you?

> Ever hit you so hard that you had marks or were injured?

Did an adult or person at least 5 years older than you ever:

> Touch or fondle you or have you touch their body in a sexual way?

Attempt or actually have oral, anal, or vaginal intercourse with you?

Did you often or very often feel that:

No one in your family loved you or thought you were important or special?

Your family didn't look out for each other, feel close to each other, or support each other?

Did you often or very often feel that:

You didn't have enough to eat, had to wear dirty clothes, and had no one to protect you?

Your parents were too drunk or high to take care of you or take you somewhere you needed to be, such as the doctor?

Were your parents separated or divorced?

Was your mother or stepmother:

Often or very often pushed, grabbed, slapped, or had something thrown at her?

Sometimes, often, or very often kicked, bitten, hit with a fist, or hit with something hard?

Ever repeatedly hit on the head for at least a few minutes or threatened with a gun or knife?

Did you live with anyone who used alcohol in a problematic way, or who used street drugs?

Was a household member depressed or mentally ill, or did a household member attempt suicide?

Did a household member go to prison?

Now add up all your "Yes" answers.
This is your ACE score.

Your ACE score isn't meant to make you feel bad about yourself. It's just a tool you can use to understand your life. Positive childhood experiences, access to community supports, and a strong network of friendships can help build resilience and protect you from some of the long-term effects of trauma. There are many people with high ACE scores who are healthy, happy, and lead successful lives.

If you are resilient, it means you have the ability to stay/become strong when something bad happens.

Read each statement and decide whether it's Definitely True, Probably True, Probably Not True, or Definitely Not True.

When I was little, other people helped my parents take care of me. These people loved me.

When I was a child, there were relatives who made me feel better when I was sad or worried.

My friends' parents like/d me.

Teachers, coaches, or cultural/spiritual leaders are there to help me when I need to talk.

Someone in my family cares about how I'm doing in school.

My family, neighbours, and friends often talk about making our lives better.

Values were talked about in our house. My parents/caregivers gave me guidance.

When I feel really bad, I can usually find someone to

talk to, and I know I can trust that person.

I seek information, guidance, and opportunities that help me live in a good way and grow as a person.

HOW MANY WERE DEFINITELY TRUE OR PROBABLY TRUE? THESE ARE THE THINGS THAT HELP PROTECT YOU. THEY CREATE RESILIENCE.

RESILIENCY IS NOT THE SAME AS HEALING.

When you are resilient, you are able to survive traumatic experiences and adjust to sudden changes. Surviving is not the same as being healthy and well.

"We need to stop praising Indigenous people for being resilient in the face of colonialism, racism, and various forms of bigotry and hate. We need to focus on creating change that prevents those situations that require us to be resilient. . . . Praising resilience has become a way to absolve society of responsibility to ensure fairness, equity, and justice."

KATERI AKIWENZIE-DAMM (ANISHINAABE)

THIS IS A LOT TO READ ABOUT, THINK ABOUT, AND FEEL.

Focus on your breathing. Is it fast or slow?

Are you feeling your body? Or are you just in your head? Shake your head to clear it out!

Sit in a chair and place your feet flat on the floor or ground. If you are a person with a disability that makes it difficult to do this, sit and place a hand, foot, or the tip of a finger on a flat surface. If you use an assistive device or have mobility challenges, you can use the wheels of your chair or the bottom of your forearm crutch to touch the floor/ground.

Close your eyes and imagine your feet/hand/finger/ device moving downward, through the floors of the building to the ground, through the ground, down through the earth to the plant roots, the soil microbes, and the groundwater. Focus on this con- nection until you feel the energy in your body moving downward, connecting to the earth.

25

Breathe in slowly through your nose. Hold it for a few seconds. Let it out slowly through your mouth. How do you feel? Let yourself be in that feeling. If you feel good, stay there and enjoy it! If you feel anxious or upset, say hello to that feeling — then encourage it to move on. Imagine it passing out of you and into the earth. Now take another breath and check how you feel. Repeat as many times as you like.

This activity helps you connect with your body and notice what you're feeling. Once you notice your feelings, you can put them outside yourself. When the feelings are no longer part of you, you can look at them. They're not taking up space anymore — they are observable. What we can see, we can change.

2

IDENTITY AND CONTROL

When we are under someone else's control, submission or rebellion are often the only ways we can respond. How do we create our own identities and our own ways of being in the world?

HOW PEOPLE THINK ABOUT US CAN AFFECT WHO WE ARE.

The dominant society has created many myths and stereotypes about Indigenous peoples. These stereotypes turn us into cartoons, victims, liars, and cheats. They make us seem like we're less than human. Sometimes, Indigenous people hear/see/learn the myths and stereotypes before we know anything about our own pre-colonial cultures.

What do you learn about yourself from the way teachers, cops, caseworkers, and store owners treat you? From the way TV news portrays Indigenous peoples? From the stories your family and friends tell about you? From what you read in textbooks? From what you see/hear on social media?

Sometimes we resist inaccurate or incomplete portrayals. Sometimes we learn them so well that those labels become who we are.

SELF-IDENTITY is how we define ourselves. We form our self-identity from the way we see ourselves and the changes we make in response to peers, family, school, and other social groups. Dreams, ceremonies, and interactions with the ancestors/spirit world also help us know who we are. Our self-identity forms the basis of our self-esteem, shapes our thoughts and feelings about belonging, and tells us how we can contribute to community.

SOCIAL IDENTITY is constructed by others, so it may differ from our self-identity. It's how other people see us and label us. For example, if you have green eyes and brown hair, you may be labelled "white" by the dominant society, even though you belong to an Indigenous community. Our social identities often don't match up with the ways we define ourselves.

WHO ARE YOU? HOW ARE YOU SEEN?

A positive self-identity creates positive self-esteem. If you are proud of yourself, you will be proud of what you can do.

Young children tend to have simple, concrete self-identities and will often define themselves by their physical traits (*I have black hair*). Teenagers and young adults have a deeper self-awareness and a greater awareness of other people, and often define themselves based on their values, thoughts, and opinions (*I think racism is wrong* or *I want to give back to my community*). As they age, most people realize that they should be lifelong learners, and that their opinions are not their identity. They learn that changing their mind is part of personal growth, and that questioning their ideas does not pose a threat to their sense of self.

Your "self-concept" is your ability to have opinions and beliefs about yourself and to state those opinions and beliefs confidently and consistently, without being influenced by what other people say or think. Many Indigenous people have a negative self-concept because they've internalized common myths and stereotypes about Indigenous peoples. It's really hard to say you're smart and you contribute to society when the dominant society keeps saying something else.

Colonization has affected how Indigenous people think about themselves. This is a form of control.

1850: BLOODY ISLAND, CALIFORNIA

2 American ranchers living on Pomo territory enslave the Pomo people, "paying" them a cup of wheat per day. 5 Pomo men kill the ranchers and take food from the ranch to feed their starving village. In response, soldiers and vigilantes use cannons, field artillery, and bayonets to kill an entire village of 135 Pomo men, women, and children. The Indian Agent says, "The tribes are kept in fear on account of the indiscriminate and inhumane massacre of their people."

1885: NÔTINITOSÎPÎHK, SISISKÂCIWAN (BATTLEFORD, SASKATCHEWAN)

8 Cree men are hanged for the murder of Indian Agent Thomas Quinn at Frog Lake. Quinn enforced federal government policy to starve Indigenous people and remove them from the land. None of the Cree men had lawyers or legal advice. Doug Cuthand (Cree) says the hangings were meant to "instill fear and control in our people." The University of Regina says, "The day the hangings took place, all the Indigenous students at the Battleford Industrial School were taken out to witness the event" to "remind them what would happen if anyone made trouble with the Crown and to provide a lasting reminder of the white man's power and authority."

1971: THE PAS, MANITOBA

Helen Betty Osborne (Cree) is picked up by four men in a car. They rip her blouse and grab her breasts. Betty fights back. She is dragged out of the vehicle, beaten, and stabbed over 50 times with a screwdriver. She is not raped. She is killed for resisting. For saying no.

2019–PRESENT: WEDZIN KWA (MORICE RIVER, BRITISH COLUMBIA)

Wet'suwet'en land defenders occupy pipeline worksites and access roads on Gidimt'en clan territory in northwest BC while also using their traditional territory for ceremonial/cultural use. Federal police in tactical gear burn down camp structures and use physical force, Tasers, guns, a chainsaw, axes, and police dogs to make arrests of citizens, allies, and journalists. Canadian federal police and pipeline security continue to engage in round-the-clock surveillance and harassment of Indigenous people on unceded Indigenous territory.

This is what colonization looks like: violence, threats, fear, intimidation, and control.

When an individual or group of individuals deliberately takes control over another person through interpersonal violence (physical force, sexual control, psychological/emotional control), neglect, and/or withholding basic necessities more than once or over a long period of time (months to years), it's called complex trauma.

Complex trauma can happen after:

- captivity (hostages, prisoners of war, concentration camps)
- abuse and control in the home (domestic violence)
- childhood physical, sexual, or emotional abuse
- sexual exploitation (trafficking)

Indigenous peoples have experienced repeated acts of cruelty and terror while under colonial control. We were/are held captive on reserves/reservations, in residential/boarding schools, by colonial governments (Indian Act, Bureau of Indian Affairs), and in the education, prison, and child welfare systems.

Complex trauma has lifelong impacts on a survivor's identity. When you are under external control, you only know what the person in control tells you. It's hard to become who and what you want/need to be. Complex trauma makes people feel helpless, like they don't have any control over their lives.

It's hard to plan for the future or see yourself as having a purpose when you feel like you have no control over anything. It's easier to live in the moment and operate in survival mode.

FREEZE

Spacing out/separating from your body • Difficulty making decisions • Feeling stuck • Can't act or respond when situations happen

FLIGHT

Feelings of panic/anxiety/worry • Avoiding places, people, talking about serious issues • Can't sit still, can't relax • Always on the go, busy doing things

FIGHT

Irritable • Explosive temper, outbursts • Bully others • Can't hear other people's point of view • Difficult/dismissive • Demand perfection from others

FAWN

People pleaser • Scared to say what you really want • Difficulty saying no • Can't set boundaries • Making friends with the threat/person in control

SO ABOUT THOSE STEREOTYPES . . .

You are NOT lazy, unmotivated, unfocused, aggressive, stoic, or noble. After years of living in survival mode, you are upset and exhausted. There's a difference.

What kind of labels have colonial systems put on you?

"DANGEROUS OFFENDER" **"WARD OF THE STATE"** **"AT-RISK STUDENT"**

FACT: The number of Indigenous people in prison in Canada increased 39% between 2007 and 2016. The number of dangerous offenders went up 2x.

FACT: Indigenous students in urban schools have the highest suspension/absenteeism/dropout rates and are put into Special Education 2x more.

FACT: Indigenous children are 7% of the population of Canada, but 48% of all foster care placements. In the US, Indigenous children are put into foster care 4x more than non-Indigenous children when abuse is reported.

ndigenous people are born into resistance. It's an identity created by colonization. By the constant need to fight oppression and genocide. By the fight to be seen, heard, included, and respected.

When we create identities different from the ones that have been created for us, we are taking back our power and taking a step toward healing.

WHO WOULD YOU BE IF YOU WERE FREE?

"My mom is white and my dad is mixed Indigenous. I'm very visibly white-passing, and so is my family. My Indigenous identity was always secondary, and it put me in a position where I wasn't really sure how to identify. Especially in circle, when we always introduce ourselves as where we're from, and I just feel like I don't really know. In high school, I didn't really identify with my Indigenous identity, mostly because I fell into that small-town, racist mindset. So when I left, my first year of university, I signed up for this newsletter, and I was intrigued by the events, but I didn't feel Indigenous enough to go. The first event I went to, I was so afraid that someone was going to be like, 'Hey, you don't belong here! Why are you here?' But when I got there, it was the exact opposite. They were so happy to have me, and I just felt so welcomed, and so appreciated, and so valued, and so heard. I never really had a community back home, because of internalized racism and intergenerational trauma, so now that I'm in university, I've built that for myself. I have this foundation of super-strong Indigenous people, and they're just like family. We're all so different and we're all from different nations, and we have different stories and backgrounds, but we're all so connected. As a Two-Spirit person, I have the opportunity to walk between two worlds. As a mixed person, I have that privilege as well."

KELSEY, age 21, Northern Ontario and Toronto

Building identity helps you stay grounded. No matter what happens, you know who you are.

REVERSE POEM

By Montana

I will always be "Just a drunken Indian."
Do not try to tell me that
I will be successful in life.
There is no doubt
My future is already written, because
I have internalized the oppression. I will never think
I am more than just my trauma. And even though
My race defines my future, I know
It is not reasonable to believe
It is possible to reclaim what was taken.
I acknowledge that
I deserve the depths of oppression.
The stereotypes overpower my strength and
It is a waste of time to think
Things will change.

When you read this poem from the top down, it high-lights the struggles of many young Indigenous people around identity, stereotypes, labels, and the future. Now read the poem in the OPPOSITE direction, from bottom to top, line by line.

HOW CAN YOU REVERSE YOUR THINKING? HOW WOULD THIS CHANGE HOW YOU FEEL ABOUT YOURSELF? ABOUT LIFE? ABOUT THE FUTURE?

> "When you no longer go around accounting for yourself, making yourself understood, justifying your existence, when you no longer feel alien anywhere, you've come home. You know who you are."

WILFRED PELLETIER
(ODAWA)

- What beliefs do you have about yourself? Have they changed over time?
- Do you think there's a conflict between who you are and how the world expects you to be?
- How does the space you're in (or the place/s you're from) affect you?
- What is your connection to family? Has it changed over time?
- How do you express your identity? Do you have more than one?
- How would your friends describe you? Do you think this is accurate?
- How has your identity, and how others see you, affected what you have accomplished in life?
- What aspect of yourself are you most proud of? What would you most like to change?

- What strengthens your cultural identity? What gets in the way?
- What is one skill you are proud to use for the benefit of others?
- What is one thing you need to work on to get better at?
- Do you know your nation? Your spirit/traditional name? How could you find out?

HOW TO BUILD A POSITIVE SELF-IDENTITY

- develop healthy sleeping/eating habits and skills to manage stress
- create healthy ways to handle disappointments in life
- stop comparing yourself to other people
- tell yourself what you're good at every single day
- set boundaries for people who bring you down
- get support from family and friends (can be chosen family)
- make sure you feel valued by the adults around you (find mentors)
- commit to lifelong learning about yourself, others, the world
- develop positive values, such as self-control, honesty, responsibility, compassion, and integrity
- grow your social competencies (planning and decision-making, collaboration, conflict resolution skills, interpersonal communication)
- cultivate a sense of purpose (what you're meant to do/contribute) and a positive view of the future

If a parent/caregiver doesn't have a positive self-identity, they can't help their kids create positive identities. This is why so many young Indigenous people have negative ideas about themselves, and why they struggle with shame, self-hate, depression, and feeling alone.

IT'S NOT THEIR FAULT. IT'S NOT YOUR FAULT. IT'S A RESULT OF COLONIZATION.

"My grandma raised me. She went to a residential school. My mom went to day school, so I understand all the shame. When people asked me where I was from, I wasn't proud to say it. Then when I came to school here, I'd get emails from Indigenous Student Services inviting me, but I was like, 'No, I think when I move, I'm gonna leave that behind. Like, I don't want people to know I'm Native.' Just because I knew what that looked like for me back home. All the stigma and just the racism. So I was like, 'I think I'm gonna recreate myself when I go.' I'm in social service work, so my courses have a piece on Indigenous people. Learning in school about what happened, the history, wasn't easy, because my grandma didn't talk about it, so I was triggered, because I'm learning and placing my grandma in all these videos I'm watching. It stirred up a lot for me. But it showed me where the shame comes from. I started to see how intergenerational trauma has impacted my family, for example, the lack of affection or the secrecy. So learning about it was a big turning point for me, because I realized not everyone knows the history. If I didn't know it, I wonder how much youth in my community know, and sometimes I wonder if they question where some of the pain comes from."

MONTANA,
age 25, Shoal Lake #40 First Nation and Peterborough, Ontario

"It is my belief that we are good people and we have the desire to do good. Unfortunately, many of us are burdened with past experiences that can get in the way of us being who we truly are. For First Nations people, it is understandable that much of what we and our parents experienced as a result of residential/boarding schools and the pass system have caused us to develop deep-seated false concepts about ourselves and about life in general."

ERIC SHIRT (CREE)

42

Discussions about identity and belonging are an important part of reclaiming Indigenous governance systems. But colonial systems/thinking can interfere.

not taylor day
@kawisahawii

Blood quantum is a colonial idea enforced onto native communities in order to tear them apart, re: John A. Macdonald's 1876 Indian Act.

Being Indigenous means kinship, ties to community, family, culture, clan. It isn't the amount of "native" in your blood. Act right.

Today, 72% of Indigenous people in the US and 60% in Canada live in urban communities. Yet most people still think that Indigenous peoples live in remote communities, far away from everyone else.

TOP 5 CITIES IN CANADA AND THE US WHERE INDIGENOUS PEOPLE LIVE:

#5 Anchorage, Alaska
#4 Oklahoma City, Oklahoma
#3 Phoenix, Arizona
#2 Los Angeles, California
#1 New York, New York

#5 Calgary, Alberta
#4 Toronto, Ontario
#3 Vancouver, British Columbia
#2 Edmonton, Alberta
#1 Winnipeg, Manitoba

HOW HAVE HISTORIES OF MIGRATION AND DISPOSSESSION AFFECTED YOUR IDENTITY?

Indigenous peoples have been forcibly relocated many times, by colonial governments and corporations that wanted the land. But Indigenous people have always had agency, too. We've been moving around forever, creating community and opportunity. Indigenous identities are rooted, but never frozen.

"My journey has been about rediscovery and cultural resurgence. Community doesn't always mean blood. Over the last four years, 'family' has become the Indigenous people in Toronto with whom I've built a community. Not to take away from my blood family, because I love them and they're so important to me. But there are different levels of family and not all levels need to be blood."

KELSEY,
age 21, Northern Ontario
and Toronto

Self-identity is good. Whole people create healthy communities! But every person needs a social identity — places and groups that help us feel like we belong.

Our social identity shows us who we are in relation to other people. Social identity is made up of many things: political beliefs, social customs, language, clan, sexuality, spiritual practices, or nationhood. Shared experiences can also create a sense of belonging. When our social identity is changed, threatened, or misrepresented — as it was/is under colonization — it can make us feel alone and misunderstood.

Our social identities influence how we feel about ourselves. If we have a positive view of our social identity, we're more likely to feel good about ourselves. If we struggle with our social identity, that can have a negative impact on how we feel about ourselves.

External factors (racism, discrimination) can change how we feel about belonging to the group. Internal factors (bullying, lateral violence) from within the group can also change how we feel about belonging — and how we feel about ourselves.

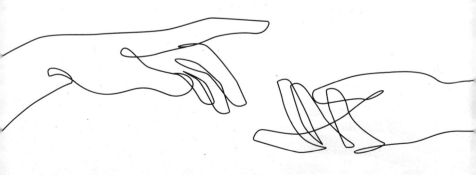

3

ISOLATION, DISCONNECTION, RECONNECTION

When we've been hurt or abused, sometimes it just feels safer to disconnect. But isolation only makes the impacts of trauma worse. Creating community with other people helps us heal.

Disconnection and a lack of self-control are dangerous threats to collective societies.

During the fur trade, the wittigo acted as a warning to Indigenous people who turned away from reciprocity and relationships and toward individualism, greed, and selfishness. Today, the wittigo is a symbol for capitalism and overconsumption. The wittigo is also part of the cycle of intergenerational trauma, where people engage in interpersonal violence within the family and politicians act with greed and selfishness or to silence people in their communities.

The wittigo also describes the forces of colonization:

- the systems, institutions, and ways of thinking that stole land, destroyed/damaged Indigenous economies, and marginalize and oppress Indigenous peoples
- contemporary government policies/practices that undermine Indigenous wellness and prosperity
- the wilful neglect of colonial governments that fail to address poverty and poor housing/health/infrastructure in Indigenous urban/rural/on-reserve/reservation communities

THE WITTIGO DESTROYS CONNECTION — TO OTHERS AND TO YOURSELF.

To kill the wittigo, we have to get rid of the negative energy that makes a person feel disconnected, isolated, and alone. We have to stop engaging in selfish, greedy behaviours that destabilize communities. We must show kindness to ourselves and others. We must live by the values of respect, responsibility, reciprocity, and relationships.

TRIGGER WARNING

This next page might be hard.

It talks about the abusive things that parents/caregivers say to us, the effect those words have on us, and the ways we manage our pain and distress.

You might want to read the next page with someone who can support you. It should be someone you feel safe with.

After the hard part, there are activities and lists that will help you stay grounded.

This part of the book shares the words of some young Indigenous people who are walking their healing path. They're going through the same things you're dealing with. Will you turn the page?

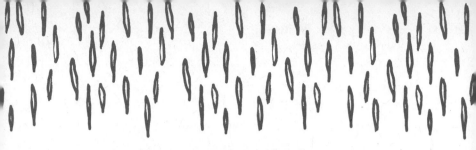

Stupid • Bad • Worthless • Ugly • No One Loves You

When you hear these words over and over as a child — from parents/caregivers, teachers, or authority figures — you learn to cope so you can get through the day. But you also learn another thing: that the people you love don't or won't or can't love you back. As you grow older, every relationship becomes like that childhood relationship: stressful and dangerous. This can make you overreact in everyday situations with friends and partners.

People with complex trauma can also feel numb sometimes. Tuning out protected you when you were a kid, but it destroys adult relationships, because you can't tell the other person what you're thinking or feeling.

WE FIRST HEARD THESE VIOLENT WORDS FROM THE COLONIZER. NOW WE SAY THEM TO EACH OTHER, ACROSS GENERATIONS.

If you experience/d trauma in childhood, you're probably good at:

- keeping secrets
- pushing people away
- acting/being mature for your age
- learning how to sense danger
- engaging in self-destructive behaviours
- not trusting people
- clinging to people, even when they're bad friends or abusive partners
- pretending you're okay even when you're not
- putting your feelings away so you can focus on surviving

IS IT HARD FOR YOU TO ASK FOR HELP?

People who experience/d childhood trauma tend to be self-reliant. We're used to going away and figuring stuff out on our own because no one gave us guidance when we were young. We often put off important tasks because we feel anxious about getting it wrong, but we don't ask for help because it's hard for us to trust people. We've been let down a lot, and not asking for help is our way of shielding ourselves from more abuse, neglect, betrayal, and disappointment. When we isolate ourselves, we're usually thinking:

"My feelings don't matter"
"I'm all alone in the world"
"I will never be enough"
"I wish I hadn't been born"
"I am a burden"

TRUTH BOMB:
You are a sacred being. Your ancestors, descendants, and spirit helpers are with you.

Dissociation is one of the most common responses to complex trauma. Feeling numb or detached is a way of seeking safety and avoiding painful feelings.

You might find yourself:

Staring at one spot, not thinking anything • Feeling numb • Feeling like you're not in your body • Feeling like you're watching yourself in a movie • Feeling like you're not part of the world around you • Feeling detached and far away from other people • Feeling like your body is foreign or doesn't belong to you • Never feeling tired/always wanting to sleep • Not being able to describe in words how your body/mind/spirit feels

We dissociate to block out distressing feelings, so we don't have to think about what happened.

There are many ways to dissociate from your thoughts and feelings:

- excessive use of social media (endless, mindless scrolling)
- binge drinking every weekend when you're away from school/work
- excessive/mindless eating even when you're not hungry

- compulsive exercising to reach a goal you're never satisfied with
- always seeking out other people so you're never alone
- being uncomfortable if you have nothing to do (always having projects)
- compulsive online shopping/gambling until you get into debt
- using street drugs, prescription drugs, and alcohol

Dissociation is about detaching yourself from the present moment. It's about escaping when there is no escape.

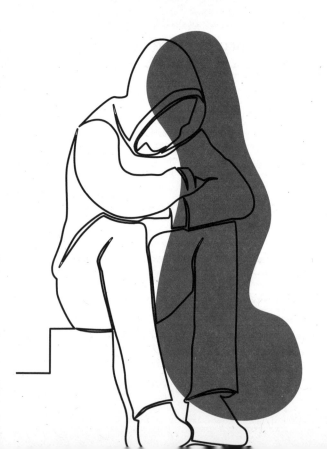

Hypervigilance is another common response to complex trauma. When you're hypervigilant, you are always on alert, watching for the next threat.

Hypervigilance can look different in different situations:

Anxiety • Unpredictable moments of rage or irritability • Hypersensitivity to confusion, disarray, or any sort of change • Pickiness about details • Talking fast, stuttering, stumbling over words • Feeling nervous, restless, tense • Sense of impending danger, panic, doom • Increased heart rate • Breathing rapidly (hyperventilating) • Sweating • Trembling • Feeling weak or tired • Trouble concentrating on anything other than the present issue/worry/thought/task • Headache • Upset stomach

Growing up in an unpredictable household (birth or foster) can often create hypervigilance later in life. Kids who aren't sure if their parents/caregivers are going to be there, if their parents/caregivers are going to be sober, or if their parents/caregivers are going to be angry have to constantly be on alert so they can stay safe. Kids who don't have regular meals or who move a lot on short notice might start fearing the loss of things they want/need. They might also be anxious and worry about the future. Kids whose parents/caregivers have unpredictable moods (sometimes loving and present, sometimes angry and disconnected) will develop into adults who worry if someone doesn't respond quickly enough to a text or email. Kids who have unpredictable lives often grow into adults who anticipate worst-case scenarios in every situation.

When a child cries and their distress is met with food or comfort, it teaches them that the world is a safe place filled with people who will help them when they ask. They learn that they get help when they tell other people how they are feeling. They learn that connection (to their bodies and to other people) helps them feel better. They feel seen and heard.

When a child cries and does not get a response — or when their cries are met with abuse — they learn that the world is an unsafe place and that no one will help them. They learn that there is no point in telling anyone how they feel. They don't learn how to describe their feelings, so they don't develop a body–mind connection. They feel isolated and misunderstood.

Next time you judge, criticize, or blame someone, ask yourself: What feelings inside of myself am I avoiding by turning my focus to other people?

Next time you feel jealousy, anger, fear, or self-pity, ask yourself: What core belief is underneath this feeling?

THE IDEAS YOU HAVE ABOUT YOURSELF, OTHER PEOPLE, AND THE WORLD COME FROM SOMEWHERE.

If we feel abandoned or not worthy of love, we feel invisible. We live in fear of the next abandonment. It's hard for us to feel curious, playful, or at ease. It's hard for us to create relationships with other people.

When we are soothed by our parent/caregiver, we develop a bond (attachment). When we are attached to our parent/caregiver, we feel secure knowing that we can explore the world and return to that safe place at any time for care and comfort.

When we are not soothed by our parent/caregiver, we feel small and insignificant. This creates shame and self-doubt. Our brains never produce the "feel good" chemicals that happen when we bond with another person. Many survivors use opiates to produce that feeling instead.

"I definitely have felt anxiety and sadness, and I don't know how to handle it. I don't know who to talk to, you know? Sports help me get out of that head space so I don't really think about the negative things. I'm in basketball, so I do that from 3 to 5 and then I go to the Friendship Centre and play from 7 to 9. The more I'm alone, that's when I start to think about things, and I start to wonder, 'Well, what about this, and what about that.' I feel like basketball separates me from all of the stress. It definitely boosts my confidence and makes me feel better about myself. When I graduate, I want to do something with Indigenous healthcare, like work in a methadone clinic. That's an issue, and I really want to work on it to make it better for the future. Not just for people that I might care about, but also for other people. Some people might wonder, 'Why am I feeling like this? This is wrong,' but it isn't. It's normal. You're not the only one."

KENNEDY,
age 16, Flying Post #72 First Nation and Timmins, Ontario

Survivors of childhood trauma can sometimes be difficult people: angry, defensive, oppositional. These are survival strategies aimed at pushing people away. When you have experienced prolonged or repeated trauma, your nervous system stays on alert. You never feel safe, even when you're away from the source of the harm. So you push people away because you're afraid of being hurt again.

Our survival skills are defensive weapons. Keeping people away feels safer. But pushing people away also closes us off from learning and growth.

Many Indigenous nations are creating land-based programs to heal the effects of complex trauma. These programs help people learn about Indigenous histories and Indigenous ways of knowing, being, and doing. They often use Western methods alongside Indigenous approaches, too. The aim is to help people re-/connect to land, self, and community so that they can let go of survival strategies like hypervigilance and coping mechanisms including addictions. The programs aim to transform feelings of shame/self-blame/hopelessness into feelings of worth and purpose, so survivors can start living as whole human beings.

Every human being has a spiritual, biological, and psychological need for connection. The best way to combat fear and shame is to learn how to connect with other people, so you can be seen and supported.

The Walgwan Centre, in Mi'kmaq territory on the south shore of the Gaspé Peninsula, offers Indigenous youth experiencing addiction and mental health challenges the chance to start a healing journey by reconnecting to the land. The centre takes groups of young people on 10-day trips to the bush in northern Quebec, where they fish salmon, hunt moose, reconnect to pre-colonial culture, and learn to live off the land.

Through these activities, the youth build strong bonds with each other. They also build traditional knowledge by connecting with elders. The Walgwan Centre also assigns a counsellor to each participant for one-on-one sessions. Programming is focused on Indigenous cultures and histories, so young people can reclaim Indigenous identity as part of their healing journey.

In 2018, an urban land-based healing and wellness camp opened in Yellowknife, Northwest Territories. Programming and supports are available for men, women, and families. Many of the participants are experiencing homelessness. The camp features canvas bush tents, tipis, an Inuit tent, cultural tools, ancestral objects, and local traditional foods so that visitors can experience the sights, sounds, smells, and textures of a land camp. Participants can decide what they want to focus on, from a range of subjects that include cultural identity, self-esteem, agency, and coping with stress. Positive role models and community building is a big part of the programming, along with ceremonies, food prep, tool making, land/medicine teachings, sweat lodges, and cultural gatherings. The organizers of the urban healing camp didn't want to Indigenize a medical/mental health model from the dominant society. They wanted a culture-based approach, and they wanted to be self-determining. Board, staff, and support people are all Indigenous, and camp planning and governance happens through an elders' council. People who visited the healing camp say that their lives changed "in a positive way" after they visited.

SO HOW DO YOU GET OUT OF SURVIVAL MODE?

Survival mode is a reaction to complex trauma. It's supposed to be a phase that helps save your life. It's not meant to be how you live your life. Healing means getting away from survival strategies, so you can **RESPOND** instead of **REACT**.

REACTING

Done on impulse • Brain/body on autopilot • Don't think about end result • Don't consider what kind of outcome you want • Acting in opposition to a situation/person ("You hurt me, so I'll hurt you back") • Happens because you feel sad/hurt/angry about what is being said/done • Done to defend yourself

RESPONDING

Done more slowly • Connecting with how you feel • Being aware of yourself and what's around you • Exploring possible outcomes before doing/replying • Considering long-term effects and what would be best for yourself and others • Matching your response with your core values • Mindful (in the present moment and place) instead of mind full (of feelings and unresolved emotions)

IF YOU WANT TO RESPOND, YOU HAVE TO FEEL.

Breathe (slowly, deeply)

Be aware (body, mind, spirit)

Release tension (lower your shoulders)

Connect with your body (get out of your head)

Pause (wait . . . then wait some more)

Label your reaction (What am I feeling? Why?)

Choose the outcome (What do I want to happen?)

Choose a response (Here's how I'll make it happen)

Empower yourself (I'm no longer powerless/ helpless)

Grief and anger can be overwhelming emotions. When we feel sad/depressed/angry about what happens/ happened to us, we can often feel disconnected from daily life and from the people we know. Our sense of loss and betrayal makes it hard for us to carry on with regular life.

The natural world is always in a constant process of movement, transition, and transformation. Human beings must also adapt and change over time. It's not good to be stuck in one place mentally/spiritually/emotionally.

Getting unstuck happens through the body.

Try this simple exercise to reset your nervous system and get out of survival mode. This will help you live in the present moment instead of constantly repeating unresolved emotions and survival strategies from the past.

1. Sit in a chair or on the floor. Turn your head from side to side. Is it easier to turn on one direction or the other?
2. Lace your fingers together and put your hands behind your head so you're cradling your skull.
3. Move your eyes to the right without moving your head. Keep your hands in place. Hold for 30-60 seconds.
4. Bring your eyes back to the centre. You might feel the need to sigh or swallow. That's your nervous system shifting.
5. Move your eye to the left without moving your head. Your nose should still be in the centre! Hold for 30-60 seconds.
6. Bring your hands down from behind your head.
7. Turn your head from side to side as in step 1. What has changed in your body? Are you less stiff/tense? Is it easier to turn your head?

We might not always be able to control what happens to us . . . but we can control how we respond.

Controlling our emotions doesn't mean we can't be mad or sad. We're not robots! Feelings exist for a reason — to help us respond to the challenges of life. But when we experience strong feelings, we need to be aware of what we're feeling and why, so we can decide how long we will be that way. We're all accountable for our actions. If we're upset, we can't just act out and then say, "They made me do it." We have to work through our feelings, understand where they're coming from, learn to describe them, and then choose a response.

Over-responding
anxious, angry, over-whelmed, out of control

Middle Ground
feeling stressed, under pressure, but you can deal . . . it doesn't bother you too much

Under-responding
out of it, numb, spaced out, frozen

REACTING IS EMOTIONAL.

RESPONDING IS EMOTIONAL INTELLIGENCE.

Pleasure can be a simple thing . . .

waking up feeling rested

being cozy under a blanket

Or a complex thing . . .

feeling loved by friends or family

feeling like you've accomplished something

If you experience/d prolonged or repeated trauma as a child, joy and pleasure can actually start to feel uncomfortable.

When your mind/body/spirit is always in survival mode, feeling joy and pleasure feels unsafe, because joy and pleasure bring your guard down. Feeling bad often seems safer, because it's familiar and you know how to work with that feeling. Survivors of childhood trauma will often sabotage relationships and opportunities (work, school) if they start feeling too good.

When we're in survival mode, we're not living. To live, we have to play. Feeling joy and pleasure takes practice.

Indigenous approaches to healing and wellness are based on connection/ reconnection.

When warriors returned from battle . . .
When a community experienced famine . . .
When people were displaced after
war/conflict . . .

We use/d art therapy:

- sacred stories created/delivered by a knowledge keeper/artist
- masks, dance, theatre, performance

We use/d individual therapy:

- talking with an elder, medicine person, knowledge keeper, or dream interpreter
- plant medicine, doctoring

We use/d group therapy:

- talking circles, healing circles, feasts
- ceremonies (sweat lodge, shaking tent, jingle dress dances)
- community art (raising a totem pole, making a wampum belt, tanning hides, beading circles)

When the colonial government removed Indigenous people from the land, outlawed language and ceremonies, imprisoned spiritual leaders, and split families apart, Indigenous peoples were no longer able to use customary practices to heal. Today, we are reclaiming those ways.

Healing is about reconnecting mind, body, and spirit. Sometimes that brings up old/unresolved stuff, and we start feeling sad.

This is normal. It happens because we start to realize how much we (or our family) have missed out on, and how badly some people/systems/institutions/workplaces have failed us. Healing involves healthy grieving.

"My mother and her side of the family have shared stories about their experiences, and it's very sad, you know. It's heartbreaking and crazy to think that was even reality. Things like that are still occurring, and it's horrible. I like talking about the emotions. Being connected with my Indigenous spirit, and smudging, that's made a huge impact in my life. The Friendship Centre has done many things, like talking circles, so we know we're not the only ones who are feeling a certain way."

KENNEDY,
age 16, Flying Post #72 First
Nation and Timmins, Ontario

"I've started using sacred medicines in my everyday life. I smudge daily and I offer tobacco. I have cedar in my car. I listen to my body, and I take a lot of breaks, because I don't feel like it's only me living in my body. All my ancestors are here, too. I want to create a welcoming space for them. Especially last year, I was really going through a rough time back home. So I would wake up with the sun and just go to the creek and rest my feet in there. I was able to find balance within myself through the land."

KELSEY,
age 21, Northern Ontario and Toronto

Trauma makes us feel helpless, alone, and fearful. Getting reconnected teaches us how to find safety and healing.

Healing happens through connection: to the natural world, a practitioner/counsellor that you trust, a teacher, an elder, friends, a group of like-minded people, the spirit world, and your own body/mind/spirit. Connection can happen in many ways: music/dance, activism, sports, land-based activities, a concert, a 12-step group, ceremony, artmaking, and silent reflection.

Healing isn't a magical thing that happens only in "special" places. Healing can happen in the basement gathering space of an urban Indigenous organization, a rural coffee shop, a park, a school gym, an elder's house on a reserve/reservation, in a campground, and while walking home from work. It's an everyday thing that happens when you're feeling safe, able to reconnect with others, and willing to reconnect with yourself.

THE MORE YOU FEEL YOUR FEELINGS, THE EASIER IT IS TO UNDERSTAND THEM.

"It's not the lack of love. It's about not being taught how to express it, which is the result of intergenerational trauma. Affection through hugs was something I was very fortunate to receive, but I know it's because cycles were broken for me. I try my best to break cycles and to explain things to my younger cousins when they ask questions because these things are hard to navigate. I see many youth struggling with mental health and they need support, but the people who should be supporting them don't always know how, because of the effects of the trauma. We're all doing our best, and every day presents an opportunity to try again."

MONTANA,
age 25, Shoal Lake #40 First Nation and Peterborough, Ontario

Being part of a community means you have to be accountable. Accountability means taking responsibility for yourself and toward others. Responsibility creates reciprocity. Reciprocity creates safety. Creating safety is a major part of healing.

Social media can help us connect: It can introduce us to new people and new organizations. It allows us to organize. We can use it to share our thoughts/feelings and get support.

Social media can also isolate us: Trolls tell lies. People start arguments. Mobs gang up on people. Influencer photos make us feel like we aren't enough.

"In today's society, we tend to focus more on Likes and the number of followers. I think social media played a big part in my life at the beginning of high school. It was a way I would let bullies get to me and my feelings. But social media can be used in a positive way, to promote equal rights and the importance of Indigenous studies and Indigenous education. That's one reason I want to use it for good — to show it's for much more than judging other people."

KENNEDY,
age 16, Flying Post #72 First Nation
and Timmins, Ontario

"I've been really open about my recovery on social media, and my experience with drugs, because of the fact that nobody talks about it. When I started on suboxone, it was me and just a few others from our community. Now there are a lot of people on suboxone in the community. My mom is on council right now, and she has a van going in to Kenora every single day, sometimes twice a day, to take people there for suboxone and methadone. They're working on having a clinic in the community to eliminate barriers. I didn't learn about harm reduction* until I was getting clean. You know how much that would have helped me if I had known about it back then? So I try to talk about it, all the things that aren't talked about, like harm reduction. I've been asked to speak a few times, but I don't think I'm ready. I'm still finding my voice, but I think I will try eventually."

MONTANA,
age 25, Shoal Lake #40 First Nation and
Peterborough, Ontario

---

* Harm reduction refers to policies, programs, and practices that aim to reduce the health and social consequences of substance use without necessarily reducing the amount of substances the person uses.

4

LATERAL VIOLENCE

Colonization is a brutal process that violates physical, mental, and spiritual boundaries. Lateral violence happens when Indigenous peoples act out these distorted boundaries on each other.

Complex trauma is about being under someone else's control. When you're under that control, it makes it hard to show anger, because you're afraid of being punished. So some people respond by directing their anger laterally, across peer groups. Indigenous peoples often feel powerless to fight back against colonialism and abuse, so we fight among ourselves instead.

When parents harm their children, it's because they were never shown love or empathy as children. When people harm their domestic partners, it's because they no longer recognize the sacred role their partners play in the family, community, or natural world. When families and communities experience violence across generations, it is sometimes seen as "normal" and just the way things are.

LATERAL VIOLENCE IS A LEARNED BEHAVIOUR WITH ROOTS IN COLONIZATION/ COLONIALISM AND INTERGENERATIONAL TRAUMA.

THE INDIGENOUS 4 Rs

Respect • Responsibility
Reciprocity • Relationships

Indigenous peoples have survived colonization and the everyday impacts of intergenerational trauma by holding on to cultural/ceremonial knowledge despite land dispossession, cultural genocide, racism, and discrimination. Preserving family and community has been more difficult. The effects of re-education, complex trauma, and colonization have replaced the 4 Rs with toxic patterns of communication/interaction that are psychologically, emotionally, and physically abusive. Indigenous people now treat each other the same way the colonizer treats us. That means we are now doing the colonizer's work, causing pain and suffering to each other.

> "Throughout my journey, there have been a lot of people who try to knock me down, but I keep moving forward. I think it's important to find power in our differences and use it to our advantage. It's important to remember that change is collective and intersectional."

KELSEY,
age 21, Northern Ontario and Toronto

In residential/boarding/day schools, Indigenous children were encouraged to fight each other for food or rewards. Children saw abuse, learned it, and did the same things to each other. Today, the colonial government still uses the "divide and conquer" strategy to keep Indigenous peoples fighting each other (over money, land, resources, citizenship, and more). When we're fighting each other, we don't have any time or energy to fight colonialism.

That's exactly what the colonizer wants . . . to distract us from the real issues that keep us marginalized.

"I've been through it myself, and it's difficult and confusing to go through, to cope with, because you just don't know what to do. You don't know how to react to it, because it's almost like, 'Is this even reality? Is this how someone views me?' because how could somebody be so cruel? Before, it was very different, I would let it get to me. But now I feel bad for them because they feel so low that they have to make someone else feel bad about themselves. It kinda makes me sad."

KENNEDY,
age 16, Flying Post #72 First Nation and Timmins, Ontario

People who engage in lateral violence want to make their victims feel inferior, unimportant, and alone. It gives them a false sense of power and a temporary feeling of superiority to humiliate and demean the victim, erode their sense of self, undermine their ability, and convince them that they're not good at anything. This is how the colonizer treats Indigenous peoples, so some survivors of colonial violence learn/ed how to copy those tactics. Then they use those behaviours to get power they feel they don't have.

People who engage in lateral violence often attack people who are happy and successful because they don't feel happy or successful themselves. Their victims often freeze up and don't reach out for help because they feel like they're to blame or that they don't deserve help. It's an interaction created by colonial control, which has taught generations of Indigenous children to hate themselves.

Lateral violence is a cycle of jealousy, blame, and punishment caused by traumatic experiences and fuelled by unresolved emotions such as anger, fear, and self-hate.

People are often afraid to talk about lateral violence in case they are attacked for revealing what happens in the community.

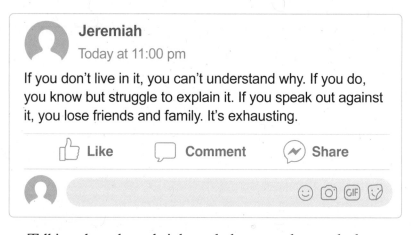

Jeremiah
Today at 11:00 pm

If you don't live in it, you can't understand why. If you do, you know but struggle to explain it. If you speak out against it, you lose friends and family. It's exhausting.

👍 Like   💬 Comment   ↩ Share

Talking about lateral violence helps us understand where it comes from and why it happens. Once we can explain it, then we can take action to stop it. The Aboriginal Peoples Television Network (APTN) did a call-in show about lateral violence in January 2020 that allowed people to share their thoughts and experiences. Constance wrote in to say that people have to "get rid of that old fearful way of thinking." Gracie said, "Teaching self-worth begins at a young age. They need role models."

Singer Susan Aglukark (Inuk) has decided to talk openly about lateral violence.

Susan says that lateral violence often takes the form of lies spread in the community or online in an attempt to shame, embarrass, or exclude the victim. The violence can also take the form of negativity and criticism. Susan says she responds with empathy, by trying "to understand why that person is behaving that way."

Susan Aglukark
Yesterday at 8:19 am

We all have been targeted for lateral violence, let's share an experience but also how we have combatted the effect, no names, no details, I'll start:

I've heard many lies about me shared and these lies get spread in the community.

Negative effect — I don't know who has heard these lies so I avoid too much contact with many people so that I don't have to deflect embarrassment and shame.

How I protect myself — I think on the lie and its possible effect and not the person lying and I try to understand why that person is behaving that way — BUT —

We also have to create healthy boundaries for ourselves — I listen to my inner voice and when I don't have emotional energy to deflect I take a break and enjoy some alone time.

 Like   Comment   Share

Susan's post got a lot of comments:

Sylvia

They know they have done wrong, but when confronted they turn around and act the victim.

Bill

I have faith that good people know the difference when perpetrators tell lies.

Mary

Being lied to and lied about has always been a part of my life. When I was young, I didn't think of what my foolishness did to others. I know now that I was numb. The land is what really helped me forgive others and to see that they too are hurting inside.

Amanda

When I've shared my knowledge or thoughts on a matter, community members become jealous or self-conscious. I'm not sure where it comes from, because it's not in any way directed towards them. I take that as part of my cue to let it go. I like discussions, and I try to find safe spaces to express myself. I just move on from the ones who are not free to learn or to teach me.

Kelly

I am glad you are speaking up. The backlash has less to do with you and more to do with them.

Sandy

We take our pain and inflict it upon others, our deepest fears of being less than, being lost and judged as lacking, always lacking, from within our cultures and without. We take that pain and tear ourselves apart, tear those leading us away from the pain apart, because we're so afraid. Some days I fear we will never be free of the pain, but then I remember how strong we are. I think of our beautiful cultures and the strength in our souls. I, like you, like so many others, will keep moving forward, doing what we can to hold each other up.

Gail

I wish it would stop, but it doesn't because of people who claim 'traditional' or 'elder' and they don't walk the talk. I have had an Indigenous woman threaten to destroy me. She tried very hard, all the while garnering respect from all the others she fooled. I left the organization for that reason. We are all hurt by colonialism and we beat each other up using those rules.

Renee

Letting go of bad feelings caused by malicious words is often a painful journey. I have felt lonely when I let some people leave my life, or, more accurately, when I removed myself from their life. There is a hole where they once were, but after a while, the hole was filled by new memories created by those who love and support me. It's a journey on a new path.

You can deal with lateral violence by showing compassion, taking away the abuser's power by not responding, and by setting firm boundaries (telling people how you want to be treated, and leaving if that doesn't happen).

Anger has a purpose.
It's a normal reaction when you've been treated badly, or you feel frightened and vulnerable.

Anger can be healthy. It can lead to change and a positive outcome:

Indigenous people were angry that Canada celebrated the 150th anniversary of Confederation, even though half of what is now known as "Canada" is actually unceded Indigenous territory. It led to a new national conversation about Indigenous histories, experiences, and perspectives. In the US, Indigenous peoples staged protests around Columbus Day starting in the 1990s. Now, more than 8 states and 130 cities celebrate Indigenous Peoples Day instead.

Anger can also be toxic, especially if it's fuelled by unresolved grief:

Grief can be scary, because it's so deep and overwhelming. Sometimes, we just don't want to go there. But when we leave our grief unresolved, it leaves our anger unresolved too. That anger then becomes stuck inside us. Some people direct that anger outward (onto other people) and some people turn it inward (onto themselves).

If someone is carrying unresolved grief, they might use anger to cover up their feelings of helplessness and powerlessness. When they're hostile toward others, they don't have to be vulnerable. When they start arguments and try to influence other people to agree with them or back away from a discussion or conflict, it's because they don't want to be wrong. They use anger as a shield, to avoid the judgment of others.

There's a difference between anger and rage.

If we've been wronged, we feel angry. When we don't process or unpack that anger, it builds up into resentment. Rage is the action we take to retaliate against the person/thing that wronged us. It's a response to, or an expression of, the anger and resentment that we're carrying.

RAGE ISN'T ALWAYS DESTRUCTIVE, BUT IT CAN BE.

Just like anger, rage can be turned inward or outward. When we turn our rage toward ourselves, it can turn into depression or a lack of self-care. When we turn our rage onto other people, it can take the form of property damage (throwing objects or destroying things) or violence (attacking someone physically, sexually, emotionally, or verbally). These are toxic forms of rage.

Lateral violence can happen when anger and rage become toxic and are directed outward. In 2022, a healing centre was burned down on the Minegoziibe First Nation. That same year, a stabbing attack on the James Smith Cree Nation killed 9 people and injured another 18. If we look behind the violence and rage, we usually see a person who is struggling with unresolved grief. Many times, they act out of resentment toward people who are doing their own healing work, or who are helping others walk their healing path.

Do you know someone who has a rigid, fixed view of the world? They think that way to protect themselves.

Children who experience/d trauma learn to make snap decisions about what is safe and what is not. That's how they survive. Later in life, that can make them uncomfortable with uncertainty. They're used to relying on themselves and their own ideas about things, so they always have to be right. They need to control things in order to feel safe, so they're not very flexible.

Lateral violence is often perpetrated by people who have fixed ideas about people/ situations, even when evidence shows them they're wrong.

Rigid thinking is a response to complex trauma. It protects us from things that make us feel fearful, which feels safer. But dealing with things that scare us is how we grow and learn.

Yelling • Snide remarks • Starting rumours • Bosses who make themselves purposely unavailable for meetings but then blame you • Colleagues withholding information or purposely giving you the wrong information • Supervisors not giving you enough work so you feel excluded or out of the loop • Bosses complaining to other employees about you (and to you about your coworkers) • Not inviting you to meetings/gatherings/social events (isolating you)

Sabotage in the workplace is a common form of lateral violence. Perpetrators usually learn their tactics inside the home. They're re-enacting their humiliation and the ways in which they were undermined and demeaned as children, but this time, they're trying to be the winner. Take time to see the wounded child inside of them. This will help you have compassion.

Sometimes people say you're a bad person so they don't have to take responsibility for how they treat/ed you. They put the focus on you so they don't have to look at their own behaviours.

Can you tell the difference between constructive feedback, being asked for accountability, and lateral violence?

Lateral violence is:

- Malicious (done to harm someone)
- Done to humiliate/demean/exclude someone
- Repeated, persistent, and occurring over time

If your boss asks for a meeting, goes through the report you just handed in, then shows you specific places that need corrections or changes, that is not lateral violence. If your boss raises their voice in front of your colleagues, throws the report on your desk, tells you that it's unacceptable, that "I don't know why I gave you this job," then refuses to distribute the report, and does this over the entire time you work there (6 months, 2 years, 10 years . . .), that is lateral violence.

People engage in lateral violence because they have unhealthy coping skills, no social/emotional skills, and a hard time having empathy or compassion for other people.

IF SOMEONE TREATS YOU BADLY, IT'S ALWAYS ABOUT THEM. IT'S NOT ABOUT YOU.

LATERAL VIOLENCE IS ABOUT POWER.

Some perpetrators like to organize mobs. They'll set up an account/profile or make a comment that gets people bullying someone online. Or they start spreading rumours so other people will gang up on someone in the community or workplace. Then they stand back and watch what happens. They like to humiliate and control other people, because it covers up their own feelings of powerlessness. The mob then acts out the perpetrator's fear, rage, and self-hate. This allows the perpetrator to (1) feel seen/heard/understood and (2) escape the consequences of their actions. People join the mob for the same reasons, and also because they're afraid of becoming targets themselves.

Once we see what's really happening, we can see what role we play. Then we can break the cycle.

WHAT ROLE DO YOU PLAY?

BE A CYCLE BREAKER.

"I DON'T WANT ANY DRAMA!"

Rod Jeffries (Mohawk) says colonization has created "chaos addiction" in some Indigenous people. They grow up experiencing arguments and constant stress so they learn how to survive it. Chaos feels normal. Calmness, patience, and time to reflect does not.

People who are addicted to chaos need the intensity of disorder. They're living in survival mode, so they're wired for a fight, for overwork, and for crisis. They crave the adrenalin rush that comes with turmoil. When they don't have it, they feel restless, so they pick a fight. They don't like the discord itself (which is why they often get frustrated and accuse other people of creating "drama") — they're just addicted to the intense feelings.

"Writing about my feelings, writing about the way I feel, just letting it all out, so I feel like I'm done, I can breathe."

KENNEDY,
age 16, Flying Post #72 First Nation and Timmins, Ontario

TRIGGER WARNING

This next part might be hard.

We're going to talk about sexual abuse/assault in families and communities, the effects that abuse has on our mind/body/spirit, and how sexual abuse relates to youth suicide.

You might want to read this next part with someone who can support you. It should be someone you feel safe with.

At the end of this section, we'll talk about Indigenous cultural approaches to healing from violence and living in a good way, to give you hope for the future. There's also an activity that will help you understand how intergenerational trauma relates to the cycle of sexual abuse in some families/communities.

You've already invited your ancestors in. They are with you. Will you turn the page?

There is a crisis of sexual abuse/ assault in many Indigenous families/communities.
This is a form of lateral violence.

"I have been silenced so many times over my 27-year career by my own leaders who made me ilirasuk* to the point of second-guessing my voice. Our silence where you are concerned is not acceptance of your behaviour or permission to carry on. For those who want to get better, what is out there for them? How do we support them?"

SUSAN AGLUKARK
(INUK)

---

* **Ilirasuk:** Susan defines this Inuktitut word as "Made to feel an overwhelming sense of inferiority to the point of being afraid; a fear brought on by a manipulation of the spiritual part of the psyche. To be emotionally controlled to the point of feeling inadequate or not capable."

When you experience sexual abuse in childhood, or sexual assault as an adult, your boundaries are broken in a violent way. When control over your body/mind/spirit is taken away from you, it's a form of loss that can have drastic effects on your sense of self. Sexual abuse/assault changes your relationship to yourself and makes you feel powerless. You learn that other people's needs come before your own. Survivors often struggle with fear and self-doubt.

Childhood sexual abuse creates issues of trust, independence/autonomy, and self-worth.

- feeling worthless and turning your pain against yourself (cutting/harming yourself in some way, telling yourself you're a bad person)
- finding yourself in situations that are emotionally, physically, or sexually unsafe
- remaining in relationships that are harmful to you
- feeling shame and being unable to speak about what happened
- acting out your sexual abuse by becoming sexually aggressive (a predator/perpetrator) or sexually permissive (repeatedly re-victimized)

Childhood sexual abuse affects your emotional and sexual development. Instead of knowing your body as a place of pleasure, you know it as a place of pain. Sex becomes about control instead of about expressing love. You learn how to use sex as a way to get power and affection.

Sexual abuse/assault is an abuse of power. The effects ripple out into entire families and communities. Conflict, breakdown of relationships, and disconnection from culture and community are common impacts.

There is a connection between childhood sexual abuse and youth suicide. In one community in Northern Ontario, there were 9 youth suicides in one year and 100 attempts. 100% of the girls and 60% of the boys had been sexually abused at home.

1. Draw a family tree using circles/squares and connecting lines.
2. Write down the names of family members inside each shape.
3. Include as many generations as you can remember or find out.
4. In each circle/square, show the kinds of abuse that person experienced, if you know of any (e.g., sexual, physical, emotional, psychological).
5. Use words, initials, or lines/dots in different colours for each kind of abuse.
6. Do your family members talk about what happened to them? How did you/can you find out this information?

7. What patterns/connections do you see on your abuse family tree?
8. How does this help you make sense of what has happened in your family? In your community?
9. How are you coping with what's been happening in your life? Do you ever feel like just giving up?
10. Have you ever thought about suicide or tried to harm yourself?
11. How are those actions connected to your abuse family tree?
12. Is there a support group, crisis center, elder, healer, teacher, counsellor, or other trusted person you can talk to?

SHAME IS A SILENCER.
SILENCE KILLS.

SPEAK YOUR TRUTH.
GET SUPPORT. LIVE.

THIS IS A LOT TO READ ABOUT, THINK ABOUT, AND FEEL.

Focus on your breathing. Is it fast or slow? Are you feeling your body? Or are you just in your head? Relax your jaw and move your eyes slowly from side to side, then up and down, to rebalance your nervous system.

Here's something that works:

When things get really hard, and you feel like you can't make it through the day, just focus on the next hour. If you feel like you can't make it though an hour, just focus on the next few minutes. Take slow, deep breaths. Try to connect with your body.

Your ancestors see you. Other survivors see you. You are not alone.

"The lovelessness that abounds in Aboriginal life is painful. It just hurts. We need to start being kind to one another, start treating each other like relatives and practising those principles of wahkohtowin."

MARIA CAMPBELL (MÉTIS)

SPIRIT WORLD

NATURAL WORLD

NATION

COMMUNITY

FAMILY

SELF

The Alberta Elders' Cree Dictionary defines wah-kohtowin as "the act of being related to one another." If you are practising wahkohtowin, you see yourself in kinship with creation and community. A good relative is someone who holds themselves accountable for the well-being of the people around them. Every Indigenous nation has something like this as part of their culture.

To live according to the principles of wahkohtowin means seeing yourself as:

- connected to all things
- responsible to the natural world
- responsible to the spirit world
- accountable to your ancestors and descendants
- playing a positive role in your community

Everything we do in life — including how we act toward other people — has an effect on the world around us. If we want to create harmonious energy in the universe, we have to consider the actions we take and the effect those actions will have on our kinship relations. We must be responsible to our relations and live our lives in a meaningful way. That means showing love, supporting each other, working together, and understanding the sacredness of all life (including our own). The relationships wheel on the previous page is one way of understanding our kinship relations.

LATERAL VIOLENCE IS WITTIGO ENERGY.

When people come together to live in peace and harmony, it is called wetaskiwin in the Cree language. Cree elder Isaac Chamakese says, "There is a lot of confusion today. People do not love each other like they should. People fight too much, they do not use wetaskiwin. We have to go back to our old ways, as Native people. We have to go back to being more loving."

What energy will you grow and share? Wittigo energy or wetaskiwin?

PRACTICE LATERAL KINDNESS

- believe in possibility (both people and communities)
- be empathetic, compassionate, and kind
- create positive feelings and positive environments
- accept responsibility for building community
- see the good in other people
- build safety and trust through genuine care

Lateral kindness DOES NOT mean that we only say and do things that other people like! It DOES NOT mean that we don't speak up, ask for help, or ask for accountability. It does mean staying aware of our own issues/behaviours. It does mean caring for one another even when it's inconvenient.

"My friends, we feel comfortable to say whatever we feel. I think it's important to be around people like that, because I don't feel judged or embarrassed or scared to express the way that I feel. With my two best friends, if I'm going through something, I don't hold back, because they really help me with grief. They provide me with that space, to access that."

KENNEDY, age 16, Flying Post #72
First Nation and Timmins, Ontario

IF YOU EXPERIENCE/D LATERAL VIOLENCE, YOU CAN:

- Report it (to the online platform, a teacher, or a trusted adult)
- Talk to the perpetrator and ask them to stop (if you feel safe)
- Speak with friends/family and share your feelings
- Look for information and support online or in your community (Friendship Center, community center, health center, resource center)
- Get help/advice at work (supervisor, manager, HR staff)
- Get support from a counsellor or support worker
- Speak to an elder, knowledge keeper, or community leader

Being a good relative (practising wahkohtowin) means working on yourself so that you don't engage in negative behaviours or create toxic environments. It's about making a commitment to be open and authentic. It's about making a commitment to not harm others in the way that you speak, work, and live. It's about looking for healing, instead of looking for somewhere to dump all your negative feelings.

Mutual Respect • Obligation • Responsibility

In the dominant society, people are seen as powerful when they have privilege and influence. Power means supremacy, dominance, and top-down rule over something or someone.

In Indigenous societies, power is created through connection: with the energy of the universe, with other people, with the natural world, and with the spirit world. You also create power when you connect with yourself and get to know your deepest thoughts and feelings.

When you see lateral violence, point it out. Own your power and use it for good. Don't deny your power. Don't give it to others to misuse against other people.

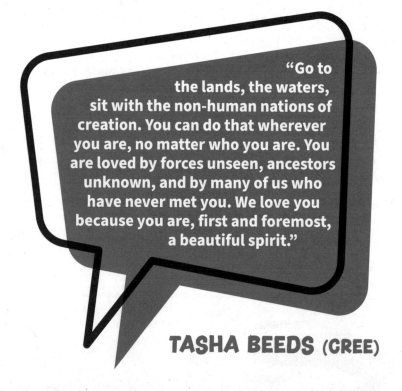

"Go to the lands, the waters, sit with the non-human nations of creation. You can do that wherever you are, no matter who you are. You are loved by forces unseen, ancestors unknown, and by many of us who have never met you. We love you because you are, first and foremost, a beautiful spirit."

TASHA BEEDS (CREE)

5

FAMILIES AND RELATIONSHIPS

Indigenous cultures survive and thrive despite colonization. But colonialism has had negative effects on our families. When you've been abandoned, abused, or wounded as a child, creating adult relationships can be really hard.

BEFORE COLONIZATION, OUR FAMILIES TAUGHT US HOW TO BE IN THE WORLD.

In pre-colonial Indigenous societies, children were strapped to their caregiver's back in cradleboards, moss bags, amautiit, or other carriers. They were in constant contact with a warm body, able to detect their caregiver's heartbeat, smell, breath rhythm, speech vibrations, and energy field. The caregiver might not turn around or take the child out for many hours. The carriers kept the child safe and calm while the caregiver was busy with their daily routine. The tight embrace of the carrier gave a feeling of security even when human touch was not available. Children developed a deep sense of self and a connection to others, paving the way for respectful kinship relations.

There is a lot of laughter and sharing in Indigenous families/communities. Elder Fred Campiou (Cree) says intergenerational trauma has also created "conflict, division, hardship, animosity, and resentment."

Patti LaBoucane-Benson (Métis) says that colonization has damaged relationships between Indigenous children and their parents and grandparents. The loss of connection and communication caused by residential/boarding/day schools, foster care, adoption, and all the other trauma of colonialism means that cultural knowledge about ethics and behaviour has not been passed down. For some families/communities, this has been happening for many generations, depending on when contact happened and colonial interference began. This silence and missing information now shapes who and how we are in the world.

When a person experiences childhood trauma, they can be overwhelmed by and unprepared for the complex demands of intimacy, caretaking, and relationship building in future relationships. If your parents never had their needs met as children, they won't know how to meet your needs. If they're in survival mode, they won't know how to be open and vulnerable with you. They might even feel triggered when you ask/expect them to meet your needs, because it might remind them of their own experiences when they were young. Being or becoming a parent can bring up a lot of unresolved emotions, including terror, anger, grief, and loss.

Does your parent/caregiver self-medicate with alcohol or drugs? Growing up with a parent who struggles with addictions means that family rules and routines are constantly changing. Things shift unexpectedly based on the moods and needs of your parent/caregiver instead of on your needs or the needs of the family. People act in unpredictable ways.

- Promises aren't kept or remembered
- Expectations vary from one day to the next (strict at times, indifferent at others)
- The same behaviour that gets you love and approval one day will get you punished the next day

Young people surviving intergenerational trauma live in two worlds: constantly monitoring for potential danger (which puts us in survival mode) and shutting down our need for love, guidance, and validation (which makes us numb). This leaves us feeling unsure, frustrated, and angry. We feel like there must be something wrong with us to make our parent/caregiver behave this way.

Kids who never get their feelings validated grow into adults who blame themselves for their loneliness and pain.

Shame → feeling responsible for doing something, feeling regret or remorse

Toxic Shame → feeling like you are flawed/ inadequate/worthless as a human being

Shame and toxic shame aren't the same. Feeling shame can actually be a good thing, because it shows you that you need to make things right again. Toxic shame is feeling bad about who you are as a person. That's never a good thing.

Toxic shame happens when other people don't treat you well, and you turn that treatment into a belief about yourself. Toxic shame is usually caused by childhood abuse and neglect.

Toxic shame makes us:

- self-critical/self-loathing (we hate ourselves)
- scared of intimate relationships
- scared of letting people know us

When we carry toxic shame, we often want to isolate ourselves and avoid people or public places. We feel like our worth as a person depends on what other people say about us, or how they treat us. Toxic shame makes it easy for us to argue away the abuse or neglect we experience/d from our parent/caregiver. We start to think that their abuse is our fault, and we develop feelings of anger, betrayal, and abandonment that damage our future relationships.

"Growing up, I saw all the addictions, all around, and I was just like, 'That's not gonna be me.' And then it was me. I started smoking weed when I was in Grade 7, which was the time I came out about the sexual abuse I experienced when I was a child. Then in high school I started drinking. After I graduated, that's when the whole sexual abuse stuff went to court, and it ended up not working out, so I just lost it. I ended up in the hospital for a while. I didn't go to school and I started drinking heavily. At that point, I was on the reserve and I was just like, 'Well fuck it, I'm just gonna be stuck on the reserve all my life,' so I ran with that. Like, that was my identity. I thought, 'I'm not going to be anything, so I might as well drink.' Then I got into a relationship but it ended up being super-toxic for the both of us. So at that point, I was like, 'Well, this is probably what I deserve.' I mean, I hated myself to the core, so nothing mattered. Eventually, I started using

prescription painkillers. I was like, 'Fuck it, I don't care. I hope it kills me.' And I started to do all the things I said I'd never do, like steal from my family and lie. I didn't value myself at all. I didn't even have a sense of self until like this year. I didn't know what I liked because I always liked what you like. I was a people pleaser. I still have a lot of work to do. The shame still comes up, like in class when they're talking about Indigenous people, I sink in my chair. As much as I used to be ashamed, and I wasn't proud, I'm totally grateful for where I come from, and all that it taught me. There is a true sense of community back home. When something happens, everyone comes out to help one another. People see all the negative things about reserves, what they don't have, but they don't acknowledge what there is. A genuine sense of community is a gift."

MONTANA,
age 25, Shoal Lake #40 First
Nation and Peterborough, Ontario

INTERPERSONAL VIOLENCE IN INDIGENOUS FAMILIES AND COMMUNITIES IS A FORM OF LATERAL VIOLENCE.

- punching
- bruising
- pulling hair
- slapping
- kicking
- biting
- choking
- throwing things
- punching walls
- kicking doors
- constant criticism
- calling you names
- taking your money
- mocking your looks
- calling you stupid
- not allowing you to eat or sleep
- using weapons to threaten to hurt you or themselves
- threatening to or actually hurting your pet/s
- trapping you in your home or keeping you from leaving
- preventing you from getting help
- abandoning you in unfamiliar places
- driving recklessly/dangerously when you're with them in the vehicle
- forcing you to use drugs or alcohol
- using subtle put-downs that are disguised as humour

Clara
Yesterday at 4:04 pm

It is especially sad and difficult to deal with when it is family bullying other family members. So the healing starts from individuals looking at themselves.

👍 Like   💬 Comment   📨 Share

Children who normalize physical or emotional abuse/neglect grow into adults who do not recognize kindness or safety.

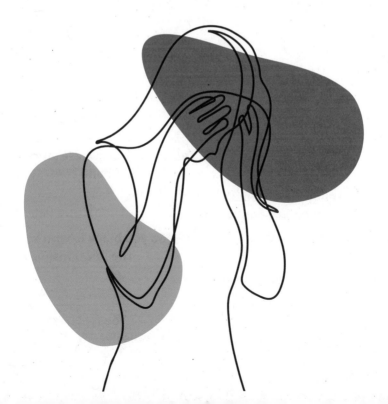

Choosing emotionally unavailable friends/ partners (the cycle)

Your parents/caregivers' love was conditional

You ignore your own feelings/ needs to try to "win over" your parents/caregivers

You see yourself as not lovable, and learn to associate love with pain and shame

You find friends/partners that make you feel the same way you did when you were a kid

You try to be perfect and ignore your own needs/feelings to take care of your friend/partner

You feel unsafe and unloved by your friend/partner (triggering unresolved feelings)

Losing loving relationships (the cycle)

You feel unsafe with parents/caregivers

You learn to associate love with danger and control

You want closeness with a partner, but fear it

So you block it/wreck the relationship

Then the relationship doesn't feel authentic

You feel unsafe (triggering unresolved feelings)

Raising children (the cycle)

You carry toxic shame from racism/discrimination/childhood trauma

Your child's needs interrupt your lifelong search for love and acceptance

You feel angry/distressed/resentful at having to take care of someone when no one has ever taken care of you

You become emotionally unavailable

You can't take care of or comfort your kids when they need it

You are accused of neglect or abuse (by colonial systems or by your child)

This creates more shame (triggering unresolved feelings)

BREAKING THE CYCLE STARTS WITH LOVING YOURSELF.

If you experience/d abuse/neglect as a child and focus/ed on survival, your relationship model looks like this:

- don't upset people because they will hurt you
- shut down to avoid pain
- don't trust others to help you or keep you safe
- control what you can
- get whatever you can get
- reject others before you are rejected
- fight your battles yourself
- charm, recruit, and manipulate others to get what you need
- make sure you have backups in case you lose someone you love
- always be ready for danger

If you have a strong, secure attachment to your parent/caregiver, your relationship model is:

- I can expect care and protection from the people I love
- I can trust my family/loved ones to be there for me
- It feels safe to be near my parent/caregiver/ family/loved ones
- I look to loved ones for safety/guidance/ validation when I'm unsure
- I communicate feelings/needs to my loved ones and can expect them to do the same

- I stay calm and can expect my loved ones to do the same when we disagree or there is conflict
- Connection, touch, and interdependence feel good

Emotional bonds in childhood give you a secure sense of self. Being secure in your self means you can create healthy, safe relationships when you get older.

ARE YOU A CARETAKER KID?

Some parents/caregivers "under-function," which means they leave their kids to take care of themselves. If you have to prepare your own meals, dress/buy/wash clothes yourself, get yourself to and from school, buy your own school supplies, and keep yourself entertained, then you are a caretaker kid. If you ever have to take care of an adult when they're drunk/high or having health or mental health challenges, then you're a caretaker kid. If you have to take care of your younger siblings because your parent/caregiver can't or won't, then you're a caretaker kid.

Caretaker kids are resilient and taking on these responsibilities at an early age teaches us skills that come in handy later in life (solving problems, having empathy . . .). But a child doesn't have enough life skills to take care of themselves or anybody else, so we start to feel inadequate. We also feel hopeless because we're stuck in a role we didn't choose. Chronic, unpredictable stress can lead to anxiety and depression. We don't feel seen, which means we lack a sense of self. Our parent's/caregiver's issues become our issues. As we age, we feel like it's our job to help, even when we're tired and need care ourselves. Other people often exploit our empathy and use us to feel good or get care. As adults, we usually don't have very good boundaries, and we lack a sense of autonomy (the feeling of existing/acting separately from others). This often makes us angry.

Being a caretaker kid is part of . . .

- **suicide crises in Indigenous communities** (feeling hopeless and wanting control over our lives)
- **academic underachievement** (not wanting to start things because we feel like we'll fail)

"You have to do good for yourself. You have to sit back and think, 'Am I okay?' and focus on mental health, making sure you're at your right spot, doing things best for you as well as for others."

KENNEDY,
age 16, Flying Post #72 First Nation and Timmins, Ontario

A child whose emotional needs are never met will grow up to see other people as sources of terror or pleasure — people who might control them, or people who might be good to them if they are "good" — but they will not see other people as individuals with their own needs or desires. This back-and-forth, all-or-nothing approach to relationships is why so many Indigenous families/communities lack emotional bonds. It's also why so many survivors of childhood trauma have problems in later relationships.

We feel distress when there is conflict because we fear being abandoned.

We have difficulty standing up for ourselves and can't set healthy boundaries.

We learn that showing needs and expressing feelings will get us hit or mocked. So we learn to push it down and disappear.

All human beings need connection. When we experience/d trauma, we go into survival mode to protect ourselves. Unlearning isolation and re-/learning how to connect is a big part of changing our relationships and healing from intergenerational trauma.

Withdrawal ← → Dependency

Complex trauma creates a lack of trust. But we're human, so we still seek the emotional connection we never or rarely experience/d in family and community. Except our childhood experiences have made us terrified of abandonment/abuse/being controlled. So we approach all relationships through a life-or-death lens, swinging between times of intense dependency/submission and terrified withdrawal/rebellion. Sometimes we seek connection in an almost aggressive way. At other times, we're distant and avoidant when we interact with other people. It's an inconsistent pattern of behaviour.

Indigenous cultural frameworks all speak about balance. The middle path is the right path to take.

Isolation is never a good thing. But being alone can be. If you don't feel like you can connect with anyone, then be with yourself. And give yourself a break if you find yourself using old behaviours again. Just because you can't change your patterns today doesn't mean you won't be able to change them tomorrow. Change takes practice.

Do you do things to please other people, without considering your own safety? Do you always look for someone to rescue you or make things better? Are there times when you don't protect yourself?

Most survivors of childhood trauma don't know what's safe and what's not, because we never learned it at home. That means we sometimes put ourselves at risk. We get into cars with people we don't know just because they ask. We drink/do drugs, stay out all night, and freeze to death. We return to abusive partners because they say they can't live without us. We stay in relationships even when our emotional needs aren't being met. We go to family gatherings even when we're bullied. We go to motel rooms because we think this time it will be different.

Talking about safety isn't about blaming the victim. It's about asking the question: How do we stay physically and emotionally safe when we don't even know what safety is?

Am I safe here? What do I really feel? Who/what am I doing this for? Am I living in the present or the past? Did my family ever teach me how to stay safe? How can I find out what "safe" feels like?

SETTING BOUNDARIES HELPS CREATE SAFETY.

"I can't do that, but I can help you find someone who can."

"I can't take on any additional responsibilities right now."

"I'm not comfortable discussing this topic with you."

"I'm uncomfortable with what you just said/did."

"Thanks for your concern, but I can handle this."

"I can't attend, but I appreciate the invitation."

"I can't give you an answer right now, so check with me later."

"Can we talk about this later? I need time to gather my thoughts."

"I need space right now, but I'll reach out when I'm ready."

"I don't feel safe, so I'm going to leave."

"I do not accept being spoken to that way."

"I'm allowed to change my mind."

"I wish I could, but I can't."

"No thank you."

"No."

Standing up for yourself doesn't make you uncooperative. Sharing your feelings doesn't make you oversensitive. Saying no doesn't make you selfish.

Being part of a family/community means you have to negotiate. You don't have to like everyone, but you do have to figure out how to live together. It helps if you can tell other people what you need.

Not-so-fun fact: Abusers never ask if the problem is them, and manipulative people never question themselves. They always say the problem is someone else. They're experts at making you doubt yourself.

"Gaslighting" is when people manipulate you by making you doubt reality and/or what's in your own head/heart/spirit.

"You need help"

"You're so emotional"

"I never did that"

"That didn't happen"

"Don't get upset over nothing"

"You're always twisting things"

"It's not a big deal"

"I was just joking"

"You're crazy"

"You're imagining things"

"You're so dramatic"

"Don't be so sensitive"

"Calm down"

"I didn't say that"

When you set boundaries and ask for accountability, some people will resist. They'll get angry and they'll probably blame you. This is because you're standing up for yourself and changing the power dynamics in the relationship.

Accountability feels like an attack to people who aren't ready to acknowledge how their behaviour harms others.

ARE YOUR FRIENDS/FAMILY TAKING CARE OF YOUR SPIRIT? THEY AREN'T IF:

- they only call when they want something
- the conversation is never equal (they only talk about themselves)
- they put you down or make fun of you in front of others
- you feel bad about yourself when you spend time with them
- they're always trying to compete with you
- they aren't happy for you when good things happen

- they bring drama into your life
- they complain about you behind your back
- your relationship feels conditional (they only love you when you're doing what they want/demand)
- they bail on you all the time when you have plans
- they use your secrets against you and share them
- they're a bad influence and make you do things that get you into trouble
- they talk about other friends/family behind their backs
- they're not there when you need them the most
- they exclude you from events with mutual friends or other family

Friends and family should be there for you no matter what. They don't judge you, put you down, or deliberately hurt your feelings. They are kind and respectful. They make you smile. They're trustworthy and they tell you the truth, even when it's hard for you to hear. They laugh with you, and comfort you when you cry. They stick around when things get tough.

HOW ARE YOUR RELATIONSHIPS WITH OTHER PEOPLE?

Pick the area on the spectrum that best describes the way you see your situation right now.

I feel completely trapped in my relationships (arguing, anger, gossiping, bullying, coercion, neglect).

Most of my relationships are harmful, not healthy.

I'm gaining an understanding of my difficult relationships. (I've started to think about how to make them better. I think more about what I'm saying/doing/feeling.)

I still have a lot of work to do to improve my relationships.

I've made a lot of progress in improving my relationships. (I think a lot about listening and talking sensitively to people.)

I see improvement in the way people respond to me.

My life is now much happier because of many good relationships. (My relationships give me peace and harmony in mind, body, spirit, and emotion.)

I am able to preserve this peace in my home and with family and friends, even when we disagree.

Don't look for the right person. Be the right person. Then your relationships will be right, too.

EVERYONE HAS A PURPOSE, AND EVERYONE SHOULD BE TREATED WITH RESPECT.

Indigenous cultures are rooted in generosity and reciprocity. Hospitality and welcome are easily seen in all communities (urban, rural, and reserve/reservation), even when the impacts of trauma are also felt on a daily basis. Sharing and togetherness makes us feel part of something. Sometimes, this makes it hard to set boundaries.

We all want to think that our family/friends/community will do their healing work, and that everyone will change and be well. The sad reality is that this doesn't usually happen. This means that you might have to walk your healing path and leave family members or old friends behind. No lie: this can be lonely sometimes. It's hard to go back to your family/community when you're doing your healing work. You want and need support, but you often don't get it. At times it feels like the toxic behaviours will drag you back down into old ways of being. Stay on your path. You won't be alone, because there are a lot of other Indigenous people who are doing the work, too.

Just because someone is family doesn't mean you have to put up with violence, chaos, manipulation, or disrespect.

Boundaries are key to all relationships

- decide what your core values are
- get in touch with your feelings
- be firm but not disrespectful/demanding
- be consistent: say what you mean and mean what you say
- practice saying no
- think ahead about how you will respond to boundary violations (what the consequences will be for people who do not respect your boundaries)

Pre-colonial Indigenous ways of knowing, being, and doing are all about healthy boundaries. This isn't something new.

"There were days when I was scared to go home, like, 'What if I relapse when I go home?' There are still some little elements where I still feel uncomfortable, so boundaries are big. But not everybody knows how to accept that. I don't let it affect my relationships with friends and family, because I recognize the things that are going on, and that they just haven't done their work yet. I've changed a lot. I realize that it's not just about me."

MONTANA, age 25, Shoal Lake #40 First Nation and Peterborough, Ontario

"Before, I was just scared. I was very scared, nervous, shy, because I didn't want to feel judged. But when I got help that provided the things I needed, then it was like, 'Okay, this isn't something I need to be backing away from. I feel comfortable now.' Relationships seem more possible now. I'm very close with my two siblings, my two sisters who are older than me. Just talking with them, I feel very comfortable to ask certain things, so definitely, they're a huge part of my life."

KENNEDY,
age 16, Flying Post #72 First Nation and Timmins, Ontario

What happens if/when you leave?

When young people leave their family/community, they are sometimes seen as abandoning the group. Many young Indigenous people find it difficult to balance personal growth, happiness, and pursuing life goals with duty, obligation, and responsibility to community.

"I don't want people to think they have to leave, like the reserve is not enough, because it is. But for me, removing myself from everything, just for a little while, was helpful. I am very grateful for my family's support, but I know that I rely on my family too much, so moving away taught me to be independent. I didn't recognize how dependent I was on outside things until I didn't have it anymore. There was a spiritual void there. All the money, drugs, alcohol, like, you take it away and you're left with you and your thoughts. I recognized that material things weren't going to help me. Accountability was a new word for me. The whole point of me leaving was to go back. But I don't know if I'm ready to go back yet. My family, they're all counting on me to be successful in school. I got funded and I feel so much pressure, especially being the first one in my family to go to college, like, 'Okay, I can't fail.' And recovery is so big. Like, I don't use drugs or alcohol or any mind-altering chemicals because I know that I will lose everything I gained in recovery if I choose to use again."

MONTANA,

age 25, Shoal Lake #40 First Nation
and Peterborough, Ontario

HEALTHY FAMILIES AREN'T PERFECT.

If you experience/d childhood trauma, you might think that other families are perfect.

Truth bomb: Every person has flaws, and every family will have times when there is bickering, misunderstanding, tension, hurt, and anger. Most families also have times when things are stressful (death in the family, money problems, illness, different expectations . . .).

Here's an easy way to tell if things are okay or not:

→ Healthy families return to normal functioning when the crisis/issue passes.
→ In dysfunctional families, the problems (and the stress) are chronic and never end.

So . . . what do healthy families look like?

- showing your feelings is allowed and accepted
- sharing your thoughts is encouraged and everyone's perspective is valued
- problems are talked about and solutions are found
- family members can ask for help and expect to receive it
- rules are made clear and are always consistent (with some flexibility to adapt to individual needs and particular situations)

Healthy families allow for individuality

Each family member is encouraged to pursue their own interests • People are free to be different • Family roles are chosen and can change over time • Boundaries between individuals are honoured

In healthy families, children are treated with respect

Children do not fear emotional, verbal, physical, or sexual abuse • Parents/caregivers can be counted on to provide care for their children • Parents/caregivers are aware of how their past experiences have affected them, and work to change any negative effects

In healthy families, children are given responsibilities appropriate to their age

Young people are not given tasks that parents should do • Young people don't have to take care of the adults

In healthy families, everyone makes mistakes, and mistakes are allowed.

We learn what to do (and what not to do) from the people around us.

Things I've learned in my family that have shaped who I am today (can be both good and bad):

Things I see/saw in my family that don't shape me as a person:

What teachings (good and bad) will you take from your family and community? What will you leave behind? What new things can you share with them?

I need you
to paint me with courage
and amplify my voice.
Breathe some light
into who I'm meant to be
and the cycles I was born to break.

By Montana

"We need role models to inspire us, so we can show pride in our cultures."

KENNEDY,
age 16, Flying Post #72 First Nation and Timmins, Ontario

TRIGGER WARNING

This next part might be hard.

We're going to talk about childhood sexual abuse and the negative effects it can have on dating relationships, sexual relationships, and sexual intimacy later in life.

You might want to read this next part with someone who can support you. It should be someone you feel safe with.

At the end of this section, we'll talk about what healthy dating/sexual relationships look like, so you have support going forward.

You've already invited your ancestors in. They are with you. Will you turn the page?

WAIT . . . WHAT?!

Why are we talking about dating and sex in the chapter on family and friend relationships? That's weird!

Well, maybe a little. But also not.

Our family are our first relationships. We learn who and how to be from inside our families. It's like what Montana says on page 106–107: what we learn and experience during childhood and as a young adult affects how we think about ourselves — and that affects our dating relationships. It's just one big, messy bunch of weirdness until you figure it all out.

SO HERE WE GO. LET'S FIGURE IT OUT.

If you experience/d childhood sexual abuse, later experiences of sex, sexual intimacy, and sexual enjoyment can sometimes be difficult.

Negotiating, developing, and maintaining sexual intimacy can be a challenge in any relationship. If you experience/d sexual abuse in childhood, it adds another layer — especially if your partner doesn't know about your childhood experiences. It can be hard to talk to your partner when you're wondering if a feeling/reaction is "normal." Then you feel isolated trying to work things out on your own.

Dissociation • Inability to be present • Feeling numb/outside your body • Inability to focus on your own pleasure • Checking out emotionally • Flashbacks • Discomfort in certain areas of your body • Difficulty feeling pleasure

To create strong sexual relationships, you need to be familiar with your body and comfortable in it. Learning how to connect with yourself is the first step. Learning how to connect with your partner and their body is the next step. Try connecting with yourself and with your partner through intimate touch first, without focusing on genitals/intercourse.

Sex, birth, and body functions are common features of Indigenous oral tradition. Trickster stories teach lessons about bodies, sex, and intimacy, usually through humour.

SH*T ABUSERS SAY
(AND WHAT IT DOES TO US)

"You're so sexy/mature, I can't help myself"
→ You feel responsible for the abuse (or
convince yourself that it wasn't abuse)

"I love you" → You confuse sex for love

"You're nothing, I can do anything I want"
→ You associate sex with being powerless
and under someone else's control, and you're
unable to be assertive about your own
needs/wants

"Don't tell" → You're unable to open up to
later partners

"You like it" → You feel shame/confusion for
being aroused (either during the abuse or in
later relationships)

If you avoid sexual activity . . .
you might be struggling with unresolved emotions
(terror, anger, fear, grief), which means sex is just too
much to deal with. Some survivors also struggle with
confusion over their sexual identity.

If you engage in lots of sexual activity . . .
you might do this to feel in control, because sexual abuse violated your boundaries and made you feel powerless. You might also think you're useful only when you're satisfying someone in a sexual way.

SEX AS ABUSE IS . . .

Addictive • An obligation • Hurtful • A condition for receiving love • "Doing to" someone • No communication • Secretive • Exploitive • Benefits one person • Emotionally distant • Unsafe • No limits • Power over someone

SEX AS POSITIVE ENERGY IS . . .

Choice • Natural drive • Nurturing • Healing • An expression of love • Sharing with someone • Communication • Private • Respectful • Mutual • Intimate • Safe • With boundaries • Empowering

Read each statement and decide whether it's a Yes or No. This will give you insight into the things you're good at, and what you need to work on.

→ I'm comfortable with my body and my sexuality

→ I can talk openly and freely with my partners and the people I date

→ I know my body and how it functions

→ I understand the responsibilities and consequences of sexual intimacy

→ I'm able to recognize risks and ways to reduce them

→ I know how to access and use healthcare services and information

→ I'm able to set boundaries when it comes to sex and dating relationships

→ I act responsibly, according to my personal values

→ I'm able to form and maintain healthy relationships that don't involve sex

If you experience/d childhood trauma, you might look for a perfect relationship when you start dating.

Truth bomb: People aren't always perfect. Relationships aren't always perfect. There will be times when you feel misunderstood, angry, or hurt. Things can be tense (money problems, poor communication, problems balancing work/school and spending time with your partner . . .).

Here are some relationship goals you can turn to when you're unsure about what you deserve and what you should ask for:

RESPECT

Treating each other as an equal and whole human being • Valuing each other's thoughts, feelings, and opinions, and working to understand them

COMMUNICATION

Talking openly, honestly, and kindly • Listening in a non-judgmental way • Affirming and valuing each other's thoughts, feelings, and opinions • Revealing your inner selves to one another by expressing feelings, thoughts about the present, and goals for the future

TRUST AND SUPPORT

Accepting each other's word and believing what the other person says • Giving the benefit of the doubt • Supporting each other's choices of activities and goals

HONESTY AND ACCOUNTABILITY

Communicating openly, truthfully, and respectfully • Acknowledging and accepting responsibility for your own actions and words • Admitting mistakes • Being reliable

EQUALITY AND FAIRNESS

Asking, not expecting • Accepting change • Making decisions together and mutually agreeing to meet each other's needs • Using a win-win strategy to manage conflict

PERSONAL TIME

Spending time together while respecting each other's need for space and privacy when needed

SAFETY

Respecting physical space • Expressing yourself non-violently, without intimidation or manipulation • Respecting boundaries • Keeping the other person's confidentiality

SEXUAL CHOICE

Talking openly about consent to sexual activities • Respecting boundaries • Making choices without pressure, intimidation, or manipulation • Talking about birth control methods • Being able to change your mind

CULTURAL AND SPIRITUAL RESPECT

Recognizing and honouring each other's cultural traditions and spiritual beliefs

In pre-colonial societies on the Plains, women owned the tipi, and they would initiate a divorce by placing their partner's clothing, moccasins, and other items outside the dwelling. Everyone struggles in their relationships! So give yourself a break as you and your partner/s learn to achieve the things on this list.

6

DIS-EASE AND SELF-CARE

Colonization has had a negative effect on the Indigenous body, including high rates of diabetes and depression. How can we use Indigenous ways of knowing, being, and doing to create well-being?

Residential/boarding/day schools have created negative health outcomes in Indigenous peoples and communities.

Widespread malnutrition in the schools prevented students from growing to their full height. It also changed their metabolism (chemical reactions in the body that change food into energy).

There is a connection between hunger, adult obesity, and diabetes.

When someone is starved, they tend to put on fat later, when food becomes available. It's because their body is in survival mode, storing energy in case they don't get food again. This means that Indigenous people who experience/d hunger are at higher risk for obesity, insulin resistance, and Type 2 diabetes.

Before colonization, Indigenous peoples ate whole foods that were high in protein, vitamins, and minerals. Today, many Indigenous people live in poverty and are forced to eat processed foods that are high in carbohydrates (sugars), salt, and unhealthy fats because they are more affordable.

OBESITY IS ACTUALLY A FORM OF MALNUTRITION.

Colonization forced Indigenous peoples to move to reserves/reservations, settlements, and cities. We went from having an active lifestyle to staying in one place and not doing much physical activity.

Loneliness also has negative effects on physical and mental health.

Poor mental and physical health can be handed down in families. Growing up in economic/emotional poverty and always being hungry/malnourished changes how our genes express themselves. This is called "epigenetics," and it's why later generations can experience the same impacts of trauma as their ancestors.

When a child is in distress and is soothed by a parent/caregiver, they develop a deep emotional attachment to that person.

When we form secure attachments in childhood, we learn how to trust what we feel. We learn how to use what we feel to understand the world around us. We learn to rely on our thoughts and feelings to respond to everyday situations. This teaches us to be okay with change. It also shows us that we can make change in the world.

When we are not attached to anyone, or we're attached to someone who abuses us, we don't learn how to trust what we feel. We don't learn how to listen to our body or how to calm ourselves down when we're in distress. Our physical sensations, emotions, and thoughts stay in disconnected fragments. We start to detach from our bodies and from the world around us. We're not comfortable inside our own selves.

Hypersensitive to criticism • Withdrawing from social activities • Feeling overwhelmed • Keeping conversation and friendships at a surface level • Being cold or distant • Being defensive/guarded • Needing a lot of down time

If you're feeling dis-ease, you're apart from the world, your self, and your reason for being.

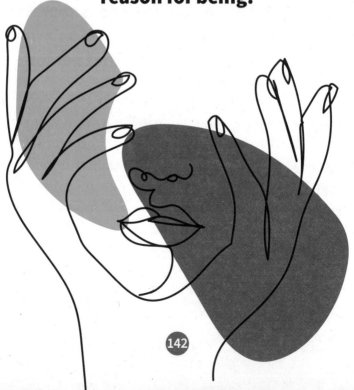

TOXIC STRESS PLAYS A BIG ROLE IN DIS-EASE.

When we are under constant stress, our hormones go haywire. Our body produces too much insulin, so we get diabetes. Our gut stops digesting properly, so we get Irritable Bowel Syndrome. When we have too much stress, we can develop kidney disease, chronic inflammation, and Polycystic Ovary Syndrome (PCOS, which can cause irregular periods, acne, thinning scalp hair, excess hair growth on the face and body, and infertility).

Inflammation usually happens when our white blood cells respond to an injury or infection. When we experience toxic stress, inflammation becomes chronic and spreads throughout the body. That can lead to arthritis, asthma, allergies, diabetes, and cancer.

Over the past few decades, Indigenous peoples in Canada and the US have gained greater self-determination in education and social services.

So here's a question:
Why is the 7th generation of Indigenous peoples after colonization so much sicker than the first?

GOOD STRESS

Brief increases in heart rate • Intensified focus •
Mild elevation of stress hormones

TOLERABLE STRESS

Serious but temporary stress response • Helped
by positive relationships • Managed
through self-care

TOXIC STRESS

Intense/prolonged activation of stress response •
No positive relationships • No self-care

Most people think that human beings have 2 nervous
systems: the sympathetic (fight or flight) and the para-
sympathetic (rest and digest).

Fact check: The human gut (esophagus, stomach, small and large intestine) has more nerve cells
than the entire spinal cord. The gut's nervous system
is independent of the other 2 nervous systems. If you
feel chronic abdominal pain and have problems with
digestion/elimination, it's a stress response. Stomach
ache, constipation, and diarrhea are your body's ways
of letting you know that there may be unresolved emotions and experiences that you need to deal with.

Listen to your body. It's telling you what you need to deal with.

Over-respond ← → Under-respond

If we experience/d complex trauma during childhood, we can often have problems dealing with the sensations/stimuli that come at us during everyday life.

Sometimes we over-respond, and are way too sensitive to sounds, smells, touch, or light. We often complain of chronic pain in different parts of our body that don't seem to have a physical/medical cause. Some of us experience multiple chemical sensitivities.

Sometimes we under-respond, and are unaware of pain, touch, or the way our body feels inside. This often means that we injure ourselves without feeling pain or develop medical/physical problems without being aware of them.

We deal with everyday life the same way we dealt with the trauma: with terror or by going numb.

We stayed alive by dissociating during the abuse, so we don't really know/trust our bodies.

Physical/sexual abuse in childhood often leads to chronic physical pain later in life.

Chronic headaches • Heart palpitations • Back pain • Stomach pain • Muscle/joint stiffness • Back pain • Vaginal/vulval irritation • Locked vaginal muscles • Erectile dysfunction

Western medical practitioners don't really understand chronic pain because they can't see it. There's no tissue damage and no physical evidence. There are no lab tests that confirm the existence of the pain. Whatever treatments a medical doctor tries will fail to stop the pain. Most times, you can't even describe the pain or explain why you're in pain. You might not even remember the traumatic incident. You just don't feel safe in your own body. You only know that something isn't right.

Many Western practitioners become frustrated with Indigenous patients who report chronic pain. We are often thought of as complainers. We're often told that our pain doesn't exist, that it's "in our heads." They don't understand that the pain is our unresolved terror, anger, fear, and loss. They don't see that mind, body, spirit, and emotion are connected.

Western medicine is often a fragmented and dehumanizing process for Indigenous people. Healthcare practitioners are seen as the experts, but most are not trauma informed.

To obtain funding for health services, on-reserve/reservation, rural, and urban communities must design their healthcare programs to match the priorities of the colonial government, instead of meeting community needs.

The colonial government makes all the decisions about what is funded. Any community engagement is advisory only.

By keeping Indigenous people sick, the colonial government makes sure that we stay marginalized. They're trying to make it impossible for us to stand up and demand our rights.

On-reserve communities in Canada get lots of dialysis machines but no help in healing from the toxic stress that's making their kidneys unwell in the first place. The machines make non-Indigenous providers wealthy. Congress consistently underfunds health services for Indigenous people in the US, which means we receive a level of care below that of federal prisoners (who are also underfunded).

GETTING WELL IS AN ACT OF DECOLONIZATION AND SELF-DETERMINATION.

Indigenous plant medicine is used for healing in communities across the Americas. But Western medical practitioners do not trust or understand this science.

Before colonization, Indigenous medicine people had knowledge that gave them political power as well. They were respected for their ability to see things and for their knowledge of how the world works. Early settlers recognized their abilities and often sought care from them. Government agents and missionaries realized that these medicine people would be a barrier to assimilation, so they took deliberate action to weaken the position of medicine people in Indigenous societies. Missionaries began to take on a leading role as spiritual advisers, and often took over the role of doctor, too. Medicine people were pushed out, elders were unable to pass on their knowledge, and Indigenous science and medicine went underground.

When Indigenous peoples get rid of colonial systems and structures that create and maintain inequality, we act as owners of our own communities. We build social capital (wealth based on people and what they bring to community, instead of on money). We create a new vision for life.

INDIGENOUS PEOPLES HAVE ALWAYS KNOWN ABOUT THE CONNECTION BETWEEN MIND, BODY, AND SPIRIT.

Your emotions live inside your physical body and are expressed as physical sensations. (Even non-Indigenous researchers agree. Google the Bodily Maps of Emotions study.) Understanding what your body is saying helps you connect to what you're thinking and feeling. This awareness is part of healing.

- Relax your shoulder/neck muscles, shake out your hands, and take 3 deep belly breaths
- Put your hands on your head and close your eyes: how is your head feeling?
- Put your hands on your heart: how is your heart feeling?
- Put your hands on your belly: how is your belly feeling?
- Put your hands on your lower back: how is your back feeling?
- Bend down and put your hands on your knees: how are your legs feeling?
- Now wiggle your toes: how are your toes feeling?
- Take a moment and reflect: how did your body feel? Did you feel anything new? Was your heart beating fast or slow? How did your hands feel on your body — cool, warm, soft, tingly?

- Now draw an outline of your body on a piece of paper
- What emotions are you feeling right now? What do they look like/feel like? Where did you feel them on/in your body? Draw them on the paper
- Are there any emotions that feel stuck/too much? Were you able to get unstuck by doing the body scan? Did drawing it help?
- Do this on a regular basis and you'll develop a better awareness of your body and your emotions . . . and what you need to work on

IS IT ADHD? OR IS IT COMPLEX TRAUMA?

23% of Indigenous children in Canada in grades 1–4 are diagnosed with attention deficit hyperactivity disorder (ADHD). Only 5% of non-Indigenous children are given that diagnosis.

Doctors in Canada and the US say that ADHD is a biological disorder with biological causes, so they treat it by changing the chemical balance in the brain with pharmaceutical drugs. Doctors in Europe say ADHD is a medical condition that has psycho-social causes from issues in a child's social environment. Instead of masking symptoms or blaming the child, they treat ADHD with psychotherapy or family therapy.

Children who experience/d trauma are often anxious, hypervigilant, numb/dissociated, sad, and preoccupied. They have trouble settling and focusing because their mind, body, and spirit are trying to manage trauma — not because there is anything "wrong" with their brain.

Studies have shown that poor diet during pregnancy and early childhood increases the risk of attention deficit issues. That makes ADHD a dis-ease caused by poverty and marginalization.

There is a link between a healthy diet and lower rates of depression and anxiety in young people.

The stomach and the brain are connected. They start out from the same cells in an embryo and communicate with each other throughout life by using the vagus nerve. The gut creates 70% of your body's neurotransmitters (chemical messengers that nerve cells use to communicate) and 95% of all serotonin. Serotonin regulates appetite, digestion, mood, social behaviour, sleep, and memory. A healthy gut keeps you feeling well.

IN INDIGENOUS CULTURES, FOOD IS MEDICINE.

In 2015, the Pueblo Food Experience project tested what would happen if people ate food from before European colonization. The 14 volunteers, who all had health issues such as diabetes, heart disease, and cancer, were examined by a doctor before and after the 3-month project. Every volunteer improved their health issues. "The industrialized food system has failed us. We shifted from economies of care to cash economies reliant on the national food system. We need to restore our food system and that ecological knowledge that has supported us since the beginning," says Acoma Pueblo farmer Aaron Lowden. Acoma is a food desert, which means that the nearest grocery store is far away (40 miles/64 kilometres to the northeast). "The closest thing is McDonald's. The food that is accessible to us is so bad for our bodies." Aaron has been teaching young people in Acoma Pueblo to farm using pre-colonial farming methods. Since 2020, over 65 young farmers have learned about seed selection/saving and how to grow corn, beans, and squash using the Three Sisters technique. The older varieties of Acoma seed have been proven to be higher in nutrition. They also need less water and are adaptable to climate change. "We are a nation here. We are not just Americans, we are Acoma," Aaron says. "A big part of keeping that sovereignty is whether you can feed your people."

Some Indigenous people are returning to pre-colonial diets made up of foods that are indigenous to the Americas (wild rice, maple syrup, berries, buckwheat, bison, quinoa . . .).

In Indigenous knowledge systems, certain foods are valued for their healing power. This healing power comes from the vitamins and minerals they contain and also from the energy they contain (sun, moon, rain, soil microbes . . .). When we eat whole foods, we bring the energy of the universe and of creation into our body.

"I'm way more conscious about what I eat. My dad hunts, and I try to only eat those meats. To be more sustainable."

KELSEY,
age 21, Northern
Ontario and Toronto

There are many ways to revive pre-colonial Indigenous food systems in urban, rural, and on-reserve/reservation communities:

Community gardens • Traditional fisheries • Food boxes • Seed saving • Food sovereignty projects • Community kitchens • Community freezers • Youth hunts • Restoring clam beds • Bison reintroduction programs

HOW CAN YOU GET INVOLVED?

Eating is a form of prayer, and a way to connect to the natural world. Mindful eating also helps with digestion.

FOCUS

Sit down if you can. If you can't sit, just stop moving. Remove all distractions (phone, TV, tablet, desktop computer, work . . .). Focus on the fact that you are about the bring the energy of the universe (soil, rain, sun, wind) into your body.

BREATHE

Take 3 slow, deep belly breaths before digging in. Now you're in your rest-and-digest nervous system. Your gut is ready to accept the gifts of the natural world and process it into nutritional energy that you can use to do your work in the world.

CONNECT

Where did this food grow/live? Who picked/harvested it? How did it get delivered to your plate? Send gratitude to the food for keeping you alive. Send gratitude to the land. Send gratitude to all the people who worked to bring this food to you.

EAT

Put the first piece of food into your mouth. Take small mouthfuls. Chew slowly. How does the food feel in your mouth? What tastes are you experiencing? Can you identify specific ingredients or combinations? Chew at least 10 times before swallowing.

Try being this mindful when you prep/cook your food, too.

The European view of the universe describes the human body as mechanical, with parts that work together like a machine. Indigenous peoples see the physical body as connected to mind, body, spirit, and emotion and to all the forces of the universe.

WESTERN MEDICINE →

- disease: a problem with the structure or function of the body
- affects a specific location/organ
- caused by mechanical failure (an organ shutting down) or external pathogen (bacteria or viruses)
- doctors treat symptoms through surgery or pharmaceutical drugs, which often have side effects
- the human body is separate from, and not affected by, the natural world
- mental health is separate from physical health

INDIGENOUS MEDICINE →

- dis-ease: when mind/body/spirit are out of balance, they turn inward, against themselves, causing problems in function

- symptoms come and go among various organs/locations in/on the body, mind, and spirit
- Indigenous medicine people ask their spirit helpers what's causing the imbalance, so they can treat the source of the dis-ease (not the symptoms)
- dis-ease is a problem of energy flow, not a problem with the structure of the body
- treatments include ceremony, drum/song, and plant medicine
- the natural world, the spirit world, and the actions of others can all affect a person's health

Indigenous peoples across the globe speak about energy. This energy is the sacred power of creation, the basic mysterious energy in/of the universe.

Energy circulates through the human body like rivers and lakes do on the earth. Energy in the natural world also circulates. When that circulation is disrupted or out of balance, dis-ease is the result. Humans are connected to the natural world and the spirit world through a constant exchange of energy.

Day/Night • Active/Receptive • Warm/Cold • Fire/Water • Masculine/Feminine • Sun/Moon

These energies are found on a spectrum throughout the natural world and inside the human body. It's a system of opposites that balance each other. Health is achieved through balance.

BTW: Two-Spirit people have always existed. They have a place in the systems of opposites, too. Two-Spirit people see/know the world through the eyes of both women and men, and the balance they represent is part of a long history of gender and sexual diversity in Indigenous communities. Before colonization, Two-Spirit people were respected and included in community life, and often did creative work or worked in helper roles (as counsellors or healers).

The human body works the same way everything else in the universe works: moving through cycles and engaging in constant transformation.

Complex trauma is about being stuck in time, stuck in past experiences, stuck in unresolved emotions.

To heal from dis-ease, we have to shift that "stuckness" and engage (or re-engage) with the world as a whole being. We have to get past the disconnection, anger, fear, and grief that trauma creates.

Intergenerational trauma is a form of blood memory. Blood memory is about presence (ancestors, spirit world) and what the late Anishinaabe scholar Gail Guthrie Valaskakis calls "goneness" (a connection to the traumatic past built through shared relationships and collective experience). Blood memory is an inheritance. It can be positive and negative. But it's not a done deal, because all energy can be shifted.

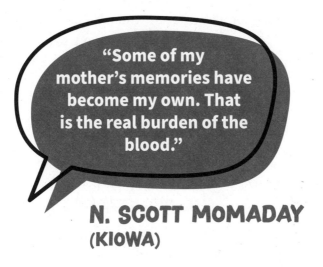

"Some of my mother's memories have become my own. That is the real burden of the blood."

N. SCOTT MOMADAY
(KIOWA)

Healing from dis-ease is about knowing yourself.

Learn how to be more aware of your body. What do you feel? Where do you feel it? What experience does it connect to?

Think about the ways that complex trauma and victimization have changed how you think about yourself. Do you think of your body as the enemy? Do you see yourself as damaged/broken? Do you think there's something "wrong" with your mind/body? This is what an abuser wants you to think. These ideas keep you weak and out of balance. That's how the wittigo moves in.

Learn how to describe what you're feeling. This is an important skill for survivors who are numb, dissociated, or disconnected from their bodies because of trauma or poor attachment. When you can describe what you're feeling, you feel more in control. You can ask for help.

Learn how to engage in self-care. Healing from dis-ease means loving yourself. That makes it easier to be accountable to your body/mind/spirit. When you engage in self-care, you develop strategies to manage feelings, stress, and disappointment. That makes you less likely to self-medicate with food, drugs, alcohol, or other distractions (work, gambling . . .).

Learn how to recognize some of the early signs of oncoming mental/physical/spiritual pain. When you're aware of your mind/body/spirit, you know what to do before the pain gets too much. Taking control will slow/stop the cycle of multiple doctor appointments, ER visits, tests, and prescriptions.

Healing from dis-ease is about shifting your energy.

In Indigenous worldviews, good health depends on:

→ social relations (connection, relatedness, obligation)
→ personal responsibility (sharing, kindness)
→ a healthy spirit (feeling joy, putting good energy into the universe)
→ the health of the land (not taking too much, living sustainably)

Using your skills to work for your community or for social/environmental/economic justice also maintains good health. When you give, you receive a lot in return.

These actions, along with healthy food, good sleep, movement, and self-care are all part of getting and staying well.

Healing from dis-ease means living in relationship with the world around you and embracing constant change. It means seeing yourself as part of creation.

YOU ARE A SACRED BEING. YOU DESERVE TO BE HERE.

Staying in balance is hard sometimes. You really have to be aware. Try the 5-4-3-2-1 exercise to connect to the world around you.

Before starting, pay attention to your breathing. Take slow, deep, belly breaths.

LOOK for 5 things around you and say them out loud. You could say "I see a pen" or "I see the sky" or "I see a spot on the ceiling."

Think of 4 things you can **FEEL** and say them out loud. You could say "I feel the pillow I'm sitting on" or "I feel my hair against my neck" or "I feel the ground under my feet."

LISTEN for 3 sounds. It could be the sound of traffic, the sound of wind on the roof, or the sound of your stomach rumbling. Say the three things out loud.

Say 2 things you can **SMELL**. If you can't smell anything at the moment, name your two favourite smells.

Say 1 thing you can **TASTE**. Maybe it's toothpaste from brushing your teeth, or the onions in the sandwich you ate for lunch. If you can't taste anything, then say your favourite thing to taste.

Take another belly breath. Reflect on the before and after. How have you changed?

If you've never been cared for, you might not know what self-care is.

PHYSICAL SELF-CARE

- ride a bike, go for a swim, play a sport, go for a walk
- get time off from school/work/home duties when you're sick
- take time to be sexual (with yourself or with a partner)
- get enough sleep, take naps
- wear clothes that you like

MENTAL SELF-CARE

- make time to be away from phone/email/apps/Internet
- listen to your inner thoughts, beliefs, attitudes, feelings
- write in a journal
- learn a new skill
- draw, paint, sew, bead, craft

EMOTIONAL SELF-CARE

- spend time with people whose company you enjoy
- make a list of 10 things you're good at
- re-read favourite books or re-watch favourite movies
- allow yourself to cry/get angry
- find things that make you laugh

SPIRITUAL SELF-CARE

- dance, sing, drum, DJ
- make time for reflection
- spend time outside
- be aware of non-material things (not money or objects)
- be open to not knowing

• • •

→ What actions do you take to care for your mind, body, and spirit in daily life?
→ What barriers stop you from starting/maintaining self-care? How could you address these barriers?
→ What negative coping strategies would you like to use less or not at all? What could you do instead?
→ Do you have land-based/cultural/artistic activities that are part of your life? How do these activities help you stay well? If you haven't had a chance to do this yet, can you ask an elder or a member of your family/community to help you?
→ What are your spiritual/religious practices? How do they support your wellness and healing?

We all feel weird or grumpy sometimes. Before you zone out, make a bad decision, or say something you regret, just **HALT**. Connect with yourself and figure out what you need. Ask yourself:

Am I **H**ungry?
Am I **A**ngry?
Am I **L**onely?
Am I **T**ired?

The HALT exercise helps us become more self-aware. It helps us see beyond the feelings and the behaviours, to the root cause of the dis-ease. That dis-ease may have started when you were a little kid and you didn't get the care you needed from the adults around you. Just remember: you're never too old for a snack or a nap.

Don't be too hard on yourself or your body. Don't blame your body for what it's trying to tell you. Dis-ease is a teacher.

Experiencing dis-ease helps us learn deep lessons about the world and our existence in it.

Why were you born into this body?

What story has your body told so far in your life?

What story is your mind/body/spirit telling you now?

Curing your dis-ease is about curing your reality. It's about making peace with your body, mind, and spirit. It's about creating a relationship between yourself and the natural world. It's about creating feelings of safety and connection. It's about creating a new sense of self.

Illness and dis-ease "not only has a history but also tells a history. It is a culmination of a lifelong history of struggle for self." (Gabor Maté, MD)

7

STORY

Stories make the world. The stories we tell (and don't tell) shape who we are and what we hope to be. Making sense of our story helps us understand past, present, and future.

Some people who experience a traumatic event have a continuous memory of it. Some have fragments and flashbacks. Others have complete amnesia.

2 factors influence memory:

→ the kind of event/s and how frequently they occur
→ the age you are when the event/s occur

If you experience/d a single traumatic event in adulthood, you will most likely remember it.

If you experience/d repeated or prolonged trauma in childhood (domestic violence, sexual abuse . . .), your memory will usually be fragmented and can sometimes intrude on daily life. The younger you are at the time of the event, the less likely you are to remember it at all.

But not remembering is a good thing, right?

Just because we don't remember something doesn't mean it doesn't affect us.

When we experience trauma, memory of the event/s are stored in the part of the brain that processes emotions and sensations but not speech or reasoning. As a result, many survivors live with sensory knowledge (sight, sound, touch, movement, smell, taste) of an event that we cannot consciously recall or describe.

Sometimes, we have mental photographs of the event — images that flash in front of us during everyday life or at night when we dream — but it's hard to make a story out of random pictures. When present-day sights, sounds, smells, and experiences create distressing feelings, not having a story means we're unable to connect those feelings to a past event. We can't make sense of what we're feeling.

But our body/spirit remembers the terror, anger, grief, and sadness of the event.

When we can't make sense of our feelings, we don't feel in control of our own mind/body/spirit. This reminds us of the original traumatic event when we also had no control.

When we feel like have no control, we dissociate to feel safe. We go numb so we don't have to feel. We use anger and rage to cover up our feelings of powerlessness.

This destroys our relationships, employment, school/studies, health, and everyday life.

When we can't create a story about a traumatic event, it's like we're living in the past.

When we have sensory knowledge of a traumatic event but no narrative memory of it, we often re-enact the event even when it causes us pain or confusion. It's like we're trying to change the outcome of the original event.

"THIS TIME I HAVE THE POWER"

"THIS TIME I'M GOING TO WIN"

Re-enacting the original traumatic event also allows us to re-experience the emotions we felt at the time. This is our way of trying to figure out or control the unresolved emotions we are experiencing in the present day.

Re-enacting past events means we often get re-victimized. Being re-victimized adds to the terror, anger, grief, and loss that we carry as Indigenous peoples under colonization.

When we're unable to create a coherent story of our traumatic experience/s . . . we carry a sense of victimization, helplessness, and betrayal. We constantly try to create explanations for these feelings, but because we don't have a story, our explanations don't really make sense. Re-enactments, or repeating the actions of an earlier event or incident, puts us in risky situations and can re-traumatize us.

When parents/caregivers/partners don't have a coherent narrative of their traumatic experience/s . . . they also carry a sense of victimization, helplessness, and betrayal. That can sometimes mean that they see themselves only as victims. They can't see that they become perpetrators when they re-enact. This leaves their children/partners at risk.

To heal from a traumatic event, we need to create a story that brings together past, present, and future.

→ Make art: let the paint/clay/colour/textile/wood absorb your energy and transform it so you can see it looking back at you
→ Write: use words that describe what happened, so you can figure it out and gain some control without putting yourself (or your loved ones) at risk
→ Dance: give your feelings to the earth or the spirit world and ask for insight
→ Sing/create music: put your feelings into the beat or use your voice to shift your energy, then take time afterward to reflect on how this has changed you

Having a story about our experience/s changes how we see ourselves. It fixes the separation between feelings, memory, and sense of self.

When we create our own stories, we own ourselves. We go from victim to survivor. We go from toxic shame to not to blame.

WHAT HAPPENED TO ME?

When did it happen?

Who was responsible for the event/s?

Who was a bystander/enabler/apologizer?

How did the event/s make me feel?

How do I feel now, talking about it?

What effect does what happened have on the way I think about myself, the world, and other people?

What effect does what happened have on my habits, behaviors, and choices?

What effect does what happened have on my family/ community?

Now we control who we are inside and who we are in relation to other people. Now we're living in the present, instead of living in the past. Now we are free to live in joy and gratitude.

Telling our own stories is one way that Indigenous peoples can be self-determining.

"The past is the past. It hurts. Why go there?"

Because you need to know:

Who am I? Who are we?

What has happened to us and our communities?

What has the world made of me that I no longer want to be?

The Networks for Change and Well-Being project brings girls together from across Canada and South Africa to talk about sexual and gender-based violence. Participant Bongiwe Maome says, "The most remarkable takeaway from being a part of this community is the gift of being able to first look inwards for positive change before expecting it to manifest outwardly. Because it is not until we hold ourselves accountable to the collective realization of positive social transformation that we can begin to see the meaningful and sustained manifestation of social change in the world around us." Hannah Battiste (Mi'kmaw) says, "Our focus was on the community, what we would want to see in the community, and what we can do to change the community. Networks for Change was not just changing our views and community, it was changing ourselves, it was changing our outlook on life."

"If you don't have a history, you don't have a future."

AKANYA NAJI/CY STANDING (DAKOTA)

The justice system in Canada recognizes the impacts of trauma on offenders, and their need to create a narrative. Section 718.2(e) of the Criminal Code allows judges to consider the life history of the offender during sentencing or after they plead guilty. This is known as the Gladue decision.

Every Indigenous offender has the right to have a Gladue report written for them by a trained Gladue writer. It's a free service.

The Gladue writer will interview you and members of your family (if possible) about your background and life experiences.

Gladue writers will ask:

- if you attended residential/boarding/day school
- if you grew up in a home where there was poverty or domestic violence
- if you were physically or sexually abused as a child
- if you were removed from home by child welfare
- if you have developmental/medical/mental health issues such as Fetal Alcohol Spectrum Disorder or addictions

Gladue reports give offenders the chance to take part in addictions treatment, anger management, life rehabilitation, elder counselling, sweat lodge ceremonies, and other programs.

Gladue reports are not a Get Out of Jail Free card. They're about getting to the root causes of why someone is in conflict with the law.

Create a timeline that represents significant events or choices in your life.

Get a piece of paper/cardboard/poster board and something to write with. Choose 5–10 events that represent your past. Choose 5 goals or events that you want to be part of your future. Draw a timeline and put the events/goals on it. If you want, choose different colours for the past and present events.

For your past, you could choose: historical events, important relationships, the way people have acted/behaved toward you (fear, conformity, prejudice, caring, loving . . .), memories, childhood experiences, school events, a special trip, an object you received from someone special, a time you hurt someone, a time someone else hurt you, a funny event, a time you cried, a hospital stay, an animal you shared an experience with, a social gathering, a teaching you received from an elder, or an image you saw in a dream.

For your future, you could choose: education goals, career possibilities, health, events you want to take part in, lifestyle, family, serving community, finding your purpose in life.

Now convert your timeline into a life map.

Take the events on your timeline and connect them somehow. There are no rules for this step! Just bring them together. You can draw arrows, roads, a bunch of islands and little boats travelling between each, or whatever you want. You can use words and pictures, or just symbols. Your life map can be:

- a road map with stop signs, green lights, detours, and construction delays
- a diagram
- a geographical map or atlas
- a maze
- a circle
- a game of snakes and ladders

The connectors should indicate how the road/path between one event and another event are connected.

Admire your creation. Reflect on it.

- What factors have influenced the choices you've made in life?
- What factors help you move forward and make progress? What factors set you back?
- Imagine your life map belongs to someone else. How do you feel about that person when you look at the life map? What values do you notice reflected in the important events?
- What leaps of faith/spirit have you taken in life? How did you overcome obstacles?
- What were the best experiences/decisions for you and why? What were the worst experiences/decisions for you and why?
- What would you change about your life map? Do you recognize any patterns?
- How are you holding on to the past? Where are you going in the future?

You might get some resistance from your family or community for wanting to tell some stories.

Families need to have stories. When families tell stories, it gives every member of the family a chance to build a shared history and create bonds of love, affection, respect, and trust. Participating in the family story-making helps children find their voice. Family members learn how to accept another person's ideas and emotions, so every member of the family feels heard. Storytelling helps explain how things happened and why things are the way they are. When families create healing stories, they reframe traumatic experiences so they have hope for the future.

"I grew up on the rez most of my life, but I wasn't aware of intergenerational trauma, because it wasn't talked about. I didn't know what had happened in my community. My family didn't talk about it. It's hard. I mean I can't go to my mom because I don't want to trigger her. My grandma, she talks in little bits, but not exactly what she went through, like, in detail. Sometimes I'm scared to ask people things because I'm scared I'll trigger them, but at the same time, not talking about it isn't helping."

MONTANA,
age 25, Shoal Lake #40 First Nation
and Peterborough, Ontario

Indigenous peoples have always made sense of the world through oral tradition. Today, many Indigenous people also write stories. Stories have power. They can transform you, teach you, and save you.

→ Which story do you or your family tell the most often about your life? What story do you or your family never tell?

→ What do you get from holding on to a story? What would you gain if you started telling another story?

→ If you hold on to an inaccurate story, what will it cost you? If you reclaim a story or create a new one, what will it bring you?

→ If you leave an inaccurate story behind, what will it change for you? If you reclaim or create a new story, what will it change for you?

But . . . how do we stay balanced and connected when we're telling stories about past harm?

"Will talking about our history hurt them or trigger me? There's strength in recognition. Speaking your truth is where healing begins."

MONTANA, age 25, Shoal Lake #40 First Nation and Peterborough, Ontario

When we're triggered, the feelings that come up slam us into the past — and maybe into a freeze-fight-flight-fawn response. It's scary because it feels like we don't have any control. But triggers are actually gifts. They tell us what we need to work on. They're experiences that we haven't talked about or worked through. They're unresolved emotions that want to be welcomed in and understood.

"Colonialism is hard to speak about, but there's no way of going forward or fixing issues unless we share and explain and focus on what can be done. For the people in my family who went to residential school, I think it's important for them to share their stories."

KENNEDY, age 16, Flying Post #72 First Nation and Timmins, Ontario

WHAT TRIGGERED ME?

If you feel triggered by something, read through this list. It will help you see what experiences/emotions are still unresolved. It will tell you what you need to work on.

- I felt powerless
- I felt judged
- I felt unheard
- I felt unsafe
- I felt excluded
- I felt blamed
- I felt disrespected
- I felt a lack of attention
- I felt like I couldn't speak the truth
- I felt uncared for
- I felt unloved
- I felt manipulated
- I felt trapped
- I felt controlled
- I felt like I was outside of my body

Don't let your triggers be in charge. When we learn how to manage triggers, we no longer feel powerless.

1. **Be aware:** Name it ("This is fear again"). Get to know each trigger as its own particular energy/response.
2. **Be curious:** Dive deep. Ask yourself what it means.
3. **Be mindful:** Ground yourself. Breathe. Make yourself aware of where you are. Connect to the earth. Tell yourself that you're safe and that you can work this out.
4. **Be kind:** Make yourself feel better. Engage in self-care. You need time and rest.
5. **Be proud:** Tell yourself "Yay me, I figured that one out!"
6. **Be supported:** Build your own support community filled with people who are supportive of the changes you're making in your life.
7. **Be truthful:** Your feelings are real. But sometimes they're not appropriate to the time/place that you're in when you're triggered. Tell yourself that you're more than your trauma and that you can step out of your woundedness.
8. **Be thoughtful:** Write in a journal, shoot some baskets, play some pool, spend some time reflecting, and figure out what the heck just happened and why. Connect past and present. Then think about your future.

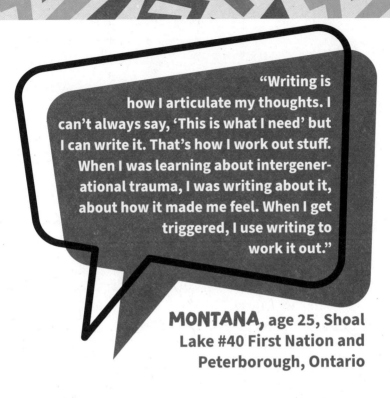

"Writing is how I articulate my thoughts. I can't always say, 'This is what I need' but I can write it. That's how I work out stuff. When I was learning about intergenerational trauma, I was writing about it, about how it made me feel. When I get triggered, I use writing to work it out."

MONTANA, age 25, Shoal Lake #40 First Nation and Peterborough, Ontario

Signs that you're healing from trauma

→ You're aware of your feelings and can describe them

→ You're not as easily triggered by people and situations

→ You're able to quickly return to a calm state after being triggered

→ Fear and helplessness start turning into feelings of confidence, connection, self-worth, and inner strength

→ Shame and self-sabotage are decreasing

→ Mistrust is replaced by openness and the ability to relate well to others

→ You're not feeling stuck anymore, and moving forward feels possible

Teach me my history
Because I need words to put to these feelings.
Because I feel the pain but cannot place the
reasons.
Because I see you hurting.
Because shame is too heavy to carry.
Because the trauma is woven in our families.
Because cycles can be broken, but first I need
the awareness.
Because I deserve to know where my strength
comes from.
Because it will heal you and I can begin to heal
myself.
Because there's so much to love, and parts of
myself I need to learn to honour.
Because learning through painful cycles hurts
more than stories.
Teach me my history
Because the truth cannot hurt me more than
colonization.

By Montana

8

SYSTEMS AND INSTITUTIONS

Indigenous people are not well served by the systems and institutions of colonial society. What does it mean to be trauma informed? Can colonial systems be Indigenized?

In 2021, youth in Iqaluit, Nunavut, marched from Inuksuk High School to the Nunavut Legislature with signs saying, "Mental health matters" and "Suicide is not the answer." They were protesting the lack of mental health supports in the North — especially around suicide prevention — and they demanded that the government build a mental health facility in Nunavut. The students said nearly every family in the territory has lost someone to suicide. Co-organizer Deion Pearce asked, "Why were we overlooked for so long? And when are we finally going to get this change?" 100 people took part in the event. Student Minnie Akeeagok, who lost her best friend to suicide, said, "This has really affected me. This is what we need to be able to move forward and get better help for youth." The youth protest started a conversation across the North about systemic change.

Indigenous peoples are asking systems and institutions to build real relationships with Indigenous peoples.

In 2022, Ryerson University changed its name to Toronto Metropolitan University (TMU) after Indigenous students, staff, and faculty voiced their concerns about attending/working at a place named after Egerton Ryerson, who helped design Canada's residential school system. A task force made 22 recommendations around how the university should deal with this colonial legacy, and one of the recommendations was to change the name. The Yellowhead Institute at TMU rebranded Ryerson as "X University" while they waited for this change. But renaming the institution is only the first step.

"X University is a very colonial institution. Its roots are embedded in racism and colonialism. It's been challenging, especially with everything that's been going on this past year, with the renaming of the university. I feel the micro-aggressions. I used to say I loved this place, but it's feeling more and more like an institution these days."

KELSEY,
age 21, Northern Ontario and Toronto

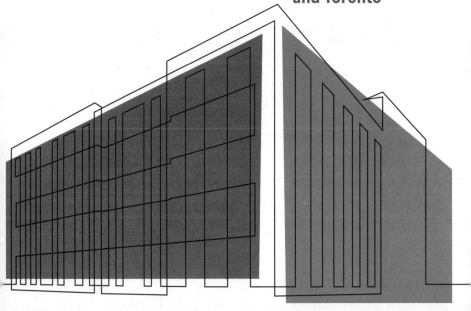

PERSPECTIVE MATTERS.

"In Social Work, we have one mandatory Indigenous class, called Aboriginal Approaches to Practice, which is good. A lot of the Indigenous classes are designed to educate settlers. Sometimes I feel like there's an expectation that Indigenous students share our experiences and trauma to educate settlers. So I feel like there should be more classes that are focused on Indigenous knowledge, wisdom, and excellence. Acknowledging Indigenous resurgence is so important."

KELSEY,
age 21, Northern Ontario and Toronto

"At my school, all the teachers who teach the Indigenous-focused courses, like Intro to Indigenous Studies, are Indigenous. It's just the other courses, like Counselling and Human Services — they all have a little segment on Indigenous people but taught by white people. It's taught to inform non-Indigenous people, but it's been super-good. They teach me a whole different perspective. So that's cool. It was helpful in my healing journey, for sure. I think it could help Indigenous people to learn their history, but in a safe environment, maybe coming from a whole different approach. I don't know what that looks like, but it has to come from us. Hearing it from someone like me, instead of from someone with power over me. It's just harder. I feel like change is possible."

MONTANA,
age 25, Shoal Lake #40 First Nation and Peterborough, Ontario

Indigenization is . . .

- understanding and using Indigenous knowledges, approaches, customary practices, and values throughout systems, institutions, and society
- including local lands, waters, and languages in the policies and daily work of colonial systems and institutions

But wait. Aren't Indigenous knowledge keepers, elders, and workers already inside the education, justice, social service, and governance systems? So why haven't those systems changed?

Decolonization is . . .

- taking away colonial approaches/ideas that have caused harm
- replacing harmful ways of doing things with equitable policies and practices that acknowledge Indigenous peoples as equal partners in society
- Indigenous cultural reclamation (restoring cultures, lands, languages, families, governance, and healthcare on our own, and with the support of non-Indigenous people)
- land back (free, prior, and informed consent under the United Nations Declaration on the Rights of Indigenous Peoples, return of unceded territories, environmental regulation, return of "Crown" lands in Canada)
- cash back (revenue sharing, compensation, payment for damages)

FACT: WE CAN'T HAVE INDIGENIZATION WITHOUT DECOLONIZATION.

In settler-colonial countries like Canada and the US, European ways of knowing, being, and doing are assumed to be the "standard" or the "norm." Other ways of knowing, being, and doing are thought of (or positioned) as "other."

This is how colonial systems and institutions establish and maintain power over Indigenous peoples. They convince us that we (and what we know and do) are somehow less worthy.

Indigenization is often approached through the lens of "inclusion." Institutions put up Indigenous art, invite Indigenous speakers in, or do a land acknowledgement, and they think the work is done. Decolonization goes way past these limited (and sometimes tokenistic) gestures of recognition. To decolonize, we have to make meaningful changes to the structure and function of systems and institutions.

IT'S ABOUT POWER, (ANTI-) OPPRESSION, AND CONTROL.

Being trauma informed isn't a specific approach, strategy, or intervention. It's not a formula. It's about the way you think, which affects what you do. It means meeting people's needs without re-traumatizing them, creating safe/empowering spaces, and supporting survivors in regaining control over their lives.

Being trauma informed means communicating and involving survivors in the process.

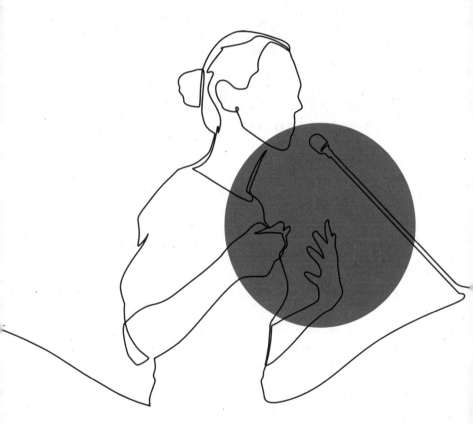

"I know that many systems and institutions were created to work against us. My experience with the justice system, for example, I see that it's broken. Victim Services, when I had to go, it took them four years, and by then I was like, 'You know what? Don't bother.' They make you watch your statement, and the process was re-traumatizing. They didn't really support me through that. The Crown told me, 'We're going to put you on the stand.' I thought this would give me some closure. So I was like, 'Yeah, okay.' I was going in with the expectation that if he didn't get jail time, at least I could share my story. But then the Crown decided, 'We don't want to re-traumatize you, so we're not going to do that, we're going to let him go' and I'm like, 'Victim Services re-traumatized me already.' I went and got drunk after that. I kinda feel resentful towards Kenora and the justice system. I feel like my voice got taken away again. That's how I feel. The voice I didn't have as a child got taken away again."

MONTANA,
age 25, Shoal Lake #40 First Nation
and Peterborough, Ontario

WHAT ABOUT INDIGENOUS SYSTEMS AND INSTITUTIONS?

Angela
Today at 3:44 pm

Chief and councils are rampant with clusters of gaslighting, scapegoating, elites.

👍 Like   💬 Comment   ⌣ Share

Many Indigenous people face challenges when they assume leadership roles. It's because they have no one to teach them what it means to be a leader. Cultural genocide and the removal of cross-generational knowledge transfer means that there are no true elders left in some communities to guide the young or advise the leadership. In some other communities, there are elders and knowledge keepers, but they are not included in the on-reserve/reservation political system, rural/municipal governance, or urban systems/organizations.

Joseph Couture (Cree) said that true elders are:

- capable of relations so that all others can equally flourish
- familiar with and able to tap into energy on a vast scale and in multiple forms (healing, creative, life-giving, sustaining)
- able to carry and use intuition, intellect, memory, imagination, emotion, humour, and a profound moral sense

194

Indigenous governance systems are based on cultural/spiritual traditions and kinship systems (clans and societies).

In most on-reserve/reservation communities, Indigenous governance systems have been replaced with elected chiefs and councils set up by colonial governments. Chiefs and councils aren't really governments — they're administrators who manage government funding/programs. They aren't given the proper resources, so they don't have the ability or capacity to address the problems, needs, and aspirations of communities.

Wilton Littlechild (Cree), a lawyer and former commissioner of the Truth and Reconciliation Commission of Canada, says that reconciliation between Indigenous peoples and the dominant colonial society must also include "reconcili-action" in these four areas:

- Spirituality must come back to leadership
- Indigenous women must take a more prominent role in leadership
- Indigenous peoples must build on their strengths
- Indigenous peoples must work to build unity within Indigenous communities

We have to return to Indigenous ways of knowing, being, and doing in order to build skills in our communities. When we fix the harm that colonization has created, we will have the power we need to fight colonial control.

"If you want change, do it yourself."
Tamara Joseph (Mi'kmaw)

When things are difficult, toxic, or not working, you have three choices: accept it, change it, or leave.

In 2018, the Assembly of First Nations (AFN) Youth Council submitted a letter to the chiefs attending the AFN annual general assembly. They asked the chiefs to reject pipelines and protect lands and waters, "ensuring a future for our young ones, and respecting our teachings." They asked for health and safety over financial gain. In response, the AFN blocked the Youth Council from speaking at the assembly. In the US, the National Indian Youth Council (NIYC) says the National Congress of American Indians is too conservative. The NIYC calls for the abolition of the Bureau of Indian Affairs and uses demonstration and confrontation as ways to create change.

In 2021, 25-year-old Tamara Joseph created the Next Generation Leadership Project in the Mi'kmaq community of Elsipogtog. Next Generation supports young people in seeking leadership positions in the community. Young people are encouraged to focus on specific areas, such as food sovereignty, disability issues, or elder advocacy. Tamara, who holds a bachelor's degree in marine biology from the University of New Brunswick, is the group's fisheries advocate. Next Generation wants a chief and council that is more engaged, transparent, and connected to community.

Jolene Crowchief says her community, the Piikani First Nation in southwestern Alberta, used to have powwows, sober dances, community hunts, and sweats. Nowadays, Jolene says that people spend a lot of time inside their homes. Jolene says community activities have been replaced with ambulances, cops, an overdose crisis, garbage, discarded needles, and abandoned houses. So she created the Hope for Healing group with her cousins Justice Yellowwings and Tori Pilling. "We can only wait around and watch things deteriorate for so long before we have to do something, because this is our home, these are our people," Tori says. The cousins call their group Hope for Healing because "we're hoping that we come back together and we unite as a community," Jolene says. Kids as young as 9 and 10 years old take part in cleanups, and Jolene says more and more people are getting involved with each event. Eventually, the group wants to build naloxone stations throughout the reserve.

The Inuktitut language dialect spoken in Rigolet, Labrador, doesn't have many fluent speakers left. When Ocean Pottle-Shiwak looked at the resources her Inuktitut teacher had, she noticed that there were dictionaries and handbooks, but none in the Rigolet dialect. So the 18-year-old created a resource book. Ocean says her great-grandfather was an Inuktitut speaker, and she wants to preserve the language for the youth of today. "I hope that it inspires a lot of younger people to know that you're not too young to help preserve your culture and advocate for your language and your people."

Schools often re-traumatize students who are experiencing trauma. Just because you're struggling doesn't mean you're failing.

Colonial trauma forces us into survival mode. When we're overwhelmed, it makes it hard to stay calm and think through all our options. It makes it hard to learn new skills or take in new information.

→ Young people who experience/d trauma can be triggered into intense reactions. In school, this looks like we're "misbehaving," arguing, or disrespecting authority.

A child who feels powerless or who grew up fearing an abusive parent/caregiver/authority figure may act aggressively or defensively if we think we're being blamed or attacked. At other times, we might be very controlled and compliant. These inconsistent behaviours make it hard to create relationships.

→ Young people who cope with trauma by dissociating seem spaced out, detached, or "out of it." We often get punished or mocked instead of getting the support we need.

INDIGENOUS STUDENTS WHO LEAVE SCHOOL ARE PUSHED OUT. THEY DON'T "DROP OUT."

Does your school board/district/ college/university have Indigenous student support workers? If not, how can you advocate for change?

"It definitely has made a difference to work with people in school. Out of everyone, the support worker 100% has made a huge impact. I feel like he understands. I don't feel judged."

KENNEDY,
age 16, Flying Post #72 First Nation and Timmins, Ontario

BEFORE COLONIZATION, INDIGENOUS ECONOMIES WERE DYNAMIC AND HIGHLY EVOLVED.

So why are Indigenous people so poor?

Indigenous trade routes once ran across the Americas. Copper was traded from Lake Superior to the Gulf of Mexico. Obsidian was traded from California to Oklahoma and the Mississippi. Textiles and pottery went from east to west. Inca traders made regular voyages up and down the coast of South America in ocean-going boats, with 20 men carrying tons of freight.

These economic systems supported small bands that travelled with the season (Plains), sedentary farming communities (Hohokam), hierarchical societies (Inca, Northwest Coast), and vast political alliances (Haudenosaunee Confederacy). Leaders and other people with wealth were expected to share what they had so that everyone enjoyed a basic standard of living. They shared a belief that land and water were relations and not commodities.

Indigenous people are poor because of land theft, Indigenous slavery, the fur trade, forced migration, broken treaties, racist/ restrictive laws, and the introduction of market capitalism.

Market capitalism is inconsistent with decolonization and healing.

In market capitalism, land is seen as private property. The complex, land-based, holistic philosophies that define Indigenous economic systems are considered primitive and irrelevant by the dominant colonial society. In the capitalist system, the natural world is used to create wealth and privilege for those in power. Shared rights and responsibilities are not important, and ownership is used to exclude others. Inequality in economic power translates into inequality in political power.

Governments and corporations in the US and Canada take billions of dollars from unceded, contested, and treaty Indigenous lands in the form of timber, petroleum, minerals, and hydroelectric resources. This money is the backbone of the settler economy. In this system, Indigenous people have two choices: join the rush for endless unsustainable upward "growth" or continue to be poor and marginalized.

Those are not valid choices. There is a middle ground with all kinds of alternative choices, including social enterprises and worker-/ member-owned co-operative business models.

The Tr'ondëk Hwëch'in Teaching and Working Farm in Dawson City, Yukon, is creating a new model for northern food security and for training and employment.

It grows vegetables and produces meat and eggs for Tr'ondëk Hwëch'in First Nations and the surrounding community using sustainable agriculture. Access to fresh food is limited in northern towns and very expensive. In spring and summer, the farm puts together food delivery boxes. They're also building an energy-efficient cold climate greenhouse so they can grow food year round. The greenhouse will provide food security so that Tr'ondëk Hwëch'in citizens don't have to depend on food trucked in from California or Alberta. The Tr'ondëk Hwëch'in farm also has teaching programs, so citizens can learn about butchering meat, growing veg from seeds, and how to grow mushrooms. Tr'ondëk Hwëch'in citizens are welcome to visit or stay at the farm for free while they learn agricultural skills (which also earns them some income). Farm manager Derrick Hastings says, "You have people staying in their community, being productive, having hope, and being part of a team effort. And then having good food, which helps people be more healthy in their minds and bodies. We want to engage with all types of citizens and give people opportunities. That creates a healthier community and healthier individuals within the community." Tr'ondëk Hwëch'in First Nations wants the farm to help people who are struggling with unstable housing and addictions.

Food sovereignty, community-led healing, and using sustainable models that reflect Indigenous cultural values are all important parts of decolonization.

Indigenous communities across the Americas are taking up their responsibility to the next 7 generations by starting sustainable development projects on their territories, including solar panels, wind turbines, and biomass.

152 projects in Canada • 190 projects in the US • Creating 15,000 person years of work • Generating $842 million in employment income

There are different forms of capitalism. We can balance economic concerns with Indigenous values. Co-operative ownership and community-led projects make sure that decision-making stays with the people and in the community.

When Indigenous people take control over infrastructure and develop community-led food, housing, and healthcare systems, it ends Indigenous dependence on colonial systems.

Community-led projects support cross-generational knowledge transfer between elders and young people.

→ 29% of Indigenous peoples in the US are under the age of 18 → 50% of the on-reserve population in Canada is under age 29

Statistics Canada says the population of Indigenous youth aged 15 to 34 increased by 39% between 2006 and 2016 (compared to 6% for non-Indigenous youth). According to the National Congress of American Indians, the median age on reservations in the US is 29 (compared to 38 for the non-Indigenous population).

YOUNG INDIGENOUS PEOPLE ARE THE FUTURE. WHAT KIND OF FUTURE DO YOU WANT THAT TO BE?

We are in a climate crisis created by colonial thinking. The Indigenous environmental/anti-pipeline movement is being led by young people, elders, women, and artists. This reclamation of Indigenous ways of knowing, being, and doing in economics and governance is a rejection of patriarchy and colonial systems.

The Indigenous environmental movement is about long-term thinking (what the impacts will be 7 generations from now). Market capitalism is about short-term thinking and the next election.

Colonialism has exposed Indigenous (and B/POC) communities to more environmental health hazards than white/class-privileged communities.

The United Nations has developed 17 Sustainable Development Goals (SDGs). The SDGs are a call to action to end poverty, protect the planet, and ensure that all people enjoy peace and prosperity by the year 2030. The SDGs are "integrated" — this means that action in one area will have outcomes in other areas.

1. no poverty
2. zero hunger
3. good health and well-being
4. quality education
5. gender equality
6. clean water and sanitation
7. affordable and clean energy
8. decent work and economic growth
9. industry, innovation, and infrastructure
10. reduced inequalities
11. sustainable cities and communities
12. responsible consumption and production
13. climate action
14. care for life below water
15. care for life on land
16. peace, justice, and strong institutions
17. partnerships for the goals

How do your life goals fit into the SDGs?

22-year-old Shay Lynn Sampson (Gitxsan) is the Youth Engagement Coordinator for Indigenous Climate Action. She lived inside a tiny house, off a forest access road, at a blockade in northern BC to try to stop the Coastal GasLink pipeline project. Shay Lynn says that "Coastal GasLink has broken or ignored hundreds of environmental assessment orders on this project. They have a terrible track record and they do not feel accountable."

Shay Lynn told the *National Observer* that "sometimes [the police] taunt and ridicule us or try to manipulate us into giving them information or giving in. Sometimes they come to destroy our freshwater containers. They arrested two hereditary chiefs and prevented them from accessing their land, which is a breach of our universal right as Indigenous people. Most recently, they have used what they call 'pain compliance' — which we call torture — on a fellow defender. . . . There has been no consent. . . . They have been asked to leave. They are trespassing."

"I grew up distant from the land. . . . I wasn't at all sure how to make sense of my place in the world. But I got involved and found my people and now it is so clear. . . . That is what waits for you when you get involved."

Shay Lynn Sampson (Gitxsan)

Can policing ever change enough to serve the needs of Indigenous peoples and communities?

In Prince Albert, Saskatchewan, 40% of the population is Indigenous. PA struggles with a high rate of serious crime, high youth mortality (15% higher than the national average), lower rates of school completion, and higher rates of absenteeism. Alcohol addiction plays a big role in negative health and social outcomes. The police in PA saw that putting people in jail was not creating a safer community, so they created a Community Mobilization Hub. Instead of responding to social disorder by taking people into custody, police in PA connect people and families to services.

After the Community Mobilization Hub was created, crime was down 37%. ER visits were down. School absenteeism was down. Hundreds of people have been diverted from jail to programs and services. But in February 2022, an Indigenous woman called police about a domestic dispute. Instead of providing her and her 13-month-old baby with help, officers arrested the mother for intoxication. The child was left at the house and later died, and the father was charged with murder. The two rookie officers at the scene were suspended, but the sergeant on duty, who other officers say was most responsible for detaining the baby's mother and not sending officers back to the house, was not. The Prince Albert Police Association says that sergeant has now been promoted to the rank of inspector and will oversee reforms to the patrol division. According to the Police Association, "We don't have any confidence. We really don't see any . . . change at the top."

Drugs, homelessness, and violent crime are now rising in Prince Albert, and more people are dying in police custody. The new police chief has faced two non-confidence votes, as well as calls for his resignation from Indigenous groups.

Is there a different model that we could use for our systems and institutions?

WHAT IS A COMMUNITY HUB?

Community hubs can be small

Parent coffee club • Youth meet-up • Community event space • After-school homework club

Community hubs can be big

Youth drop-in centre • Harm reduction services • Mental health supports • Health services • Housing services • Basic needs on demand (hot meals, out-of-the-cold program)

An Indigenous community hub could include:

Family counselling • Culture-based psychotherapy • Naturopathic doctors • Indigenous medicine people • Herbalists • Elders-in-residence • Occupational therapists • Community kitchen • Healing circles • Community art projects • Employment services • Skills-training programs • Yoga classes • MDs in a clinic setting • Dental services • Pre- and post-natal care • Library • Early childhood centre • Youth cultural programs • Art classes • Sports leagues • Community events

The integrated services in a community hub build health, wellness, and cultural knowledge. Community hubs encourage community members to collaborate with one other, which builds trust and unity.

9

CULTURE AND SPIRIT

Transforming spirit is key to healing and change. Indigenous cultural/spiritual practices have positive effects on mental and physical health.

What is healing? It's different for every person. The meaning will change at different points in the journey.

→ finding a spiritual process that includes trans-formational change and cultural renewal for people and communities

→ getting back to our original soul, the sacred being at birth

→ balancing mind, body, spirit, and emotion

→ recognizing the effects of violence, economic barriers, racism, and dispossession has had on Indigenous peoples, families, and communities

→ gaining and sustaining hope

→ developing a sense of identity and belonging

→ having a feeling of well-being, empowerment, and control

→ working toward spiritual/mental/physical renewal or wellness

→ gaining control over the direction of your life, so you can reach your full potential

→ changing community systems and improving social conditions

→ becoming joyful and open-minded/open-hearted

→ re/connecting to your needs and believing that you are worthy of having them met

→ mourning what happened to you and grieving what was taken

→ learning how to be (safely) vulnerable and connect with others

Healing is a journey. It's not an outcome or a cure. It's a process that is unique to each individual.

Healing continues throughout a person's lifetime and across generations. It's an individual and a collective process. It's about seeing, feeling, and becoming.

"To heal is to visualize what has happened to you. What are you fighting back against?"
Jeff Thomas (Urban Iroquois)

Terror, anger, and grief are overwhelming emotions. If we experience/d complex trauma, we might see ourselves as powerless or damaged. We start to feel like there's no point in planning or taking positive action. It's hard to feel hopeful. So we go back to what we know: survival mode, where we live from moment to moment and don't think about, plan for, or dream about a future.

Michael Thrasher (Cree/Métis) says that to create change, people and communities need to have these things:

- kindness and willingness
- honesty and introspection
- caring and forgiveness
- balance and creativity

Everything we do/say/think has an effect on us and on the world around us. Balance is maintained through right relationships that are founded on awareness, connection, self-control, and doing things in a good way. Some things are pre-destined (our talents and gifts, the purpose we will serve within the community in this lifetime), but we each have the power of personal agency/choice. Negative energy from other people, visitors from the spirit world, and the work of ancestors/spirit helpers can influence a person's life. But we can also change the energy around us and within us through spiritual practice. This influences the forces acting upon us.

LIFE DOESN'T GET BETTER, YOU GET BETTER.

CREATING NEW PATTERNS OF BEHAVIOUR

Here are 5 steps you can take to build awareness about the way you react in everyday situations. The aim is to replace risky or damaging behaviours with new patterns that help you feel calm and in control. Be patient and kind to yourself as you un-/learn. It takes time to develop new habits.

1. Be aware

Start paying attention to the way you react in stressful or upsetting situations. What are your old habits doing to you, your life, your relationships? Have your old habits helped you or harmed you? Notice how you feel when you act in these ways. Pay attention to how particular areas of your body feel.

2. Feel

Breathe deeply. Relax your body. Change the position you're in (move from standing to sitting or vice versa). Slow down and make some space to feel your physical self. Feel how your posture and the way your body feels connects to how you react to stressful situations.

3. Think

When you act out of habit, you're not thinking. Imagine other responses and other ways of doing/saying/thinking/being in these situations. Be creative

215

and don't limit yourself. Think using your head and your heart. If you don't know where to start, imagine how other people (characters in books/movies, people you know . . .) would act in the same situation.

4. Practice

Sometimes change feels weird. It's hard to know how to be. Don't get discouraged or self-critical if you find yourself using old habits and patterns once in a while. Think about what happened and give your mind/body/spirit time to learn new patterns. When did you become aware that you were falling into habits? What could you have done differently? Tell yourself you'll act in a different way next time.

5. Listen and reflect

What kinds of clues does your body give you when you're about to act out old habits and patterns? Learn how to listen to your body. This will help you stay aware, so you can make space for new patterns of behaviour.

"Now when something sets me off, I question myself, like 'Why?' It doesn't always happen right away, because obviously I have a lot of feelings toward it first. But I think the difference now is, I come around. And I don't feel like a victim anymore. That used to be my identity. By doing the 12 steps, it helped me see the role I have played in my own suffering and also the role I have to play in my own recovery. I looked at all my resentments, and every single one, I played a big role in. Like, 'Oh, look, there's me again!' Obviously, it's different for my abusers. I still struggle in different aspects with the sexual abuse. But in all the other things, I had to recognize my place in it first. Seeing that was super healthy. And I'm learning at school about giving names to all these behaviours, so I can see it. I'm not angry at my parents anymore, because I understand the role intergenerational trauma played in their lives. Where I used to feel anger I feel compassion now, because of the work I did. Once you know where it comes from you start to heal and understand that everyone is doing the best they can."

MONTANA,
age 25, Shoal Lake #40 First Nation
and Peterborough, Ontario

PUSH ← ... → PULL

Sometimes we return to a place that isn't good for us, just because it feels familiar. We might have connections or family there, but we don't really have the supports that we need. Creating community is an important part of healing.

KELSEY,
age 21,
Northern
Ontario and
Toronto

"I came out in 10th grade. Most of my family found out that I was queer when I was outed on social media. Being outed was really traumatic, but my family was supportive. It took a lot of courage to get where I am now, but that journey is the reason I am who I am today. I'm proud of that. Being Two-Spirit is definitely not normalized where I'm from, so that's one thing I really appreciate about the city, that people don't look at me funny when my partner and I hold hands. As opposed to back home, where people just stare and point. I feel like I really needed to create a community of queer folks in order to fully accept myself and be proud in my identity."

Courage is not the absence of fear. Courage is the willingness to live your life in spite of the fear.

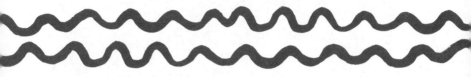

→ Half of all Indigenous people in the Americas identify as Christian
→ Some Indigenous people blend Christianity and Indigenous spiritual traditions together
→ For many Indigenous people Christianity is a colonial hangover

Indigenous spiritual traditions create and sustain community, shared values, and belonging. Some Christian congregations do this too. Some congregations only claim to do it. Forced conversion and sexual abuse by priests/nuns mean that many Indigenous people struggle with the church. In the past, there has been conflict between different Christian churches in on-reserve/reservation communities, which has resulted in factions that continue to split apart Indigenous communities today. There have also been times when churchgoers have tried to ban what they call "pagan" Indigenous ceremonies. In 2021, some churches were burned down after unmarked graves of children were found at the sites of old residential schools in Canada. Religion and spirituality is a complex issue for Indigenous peoples and communities.

"Growing up in a small community where half are Christian and the other half are 'traditional' was confusing and because of the lateral violence, I think they sometimes feel like one way is superior. So I always felt afraid to choose one, because what if I choose the wrong one? Like, what's gonna happen? I feel like it's gotten better. When they have community events they're really inclusive and make sure to honour both now. So I think we've come a long way."

MONTANA,
age 25, Shoal Lake
#40 First Nation and
Peterborough, Ontario

"I felt conflicted growing up. I didn't know how to smudge because I guess I had a colonial mindset, like there's a 'right' way to do things, and I was really afraid that I would smudge wrong. I was taught that 'you need to be clean and sober when you're doing this.' Some people think that people who are struggling need the culture in order to start healing, and some people are like, 'No, you gotta be clean before you go to the ceremony.' So I've been doing a lot of self-reflection on that."

MONTANA,
age 25, Shoal Lake
#40 First Nation and
Peterborough, Ontario

Empathy is the ability to understand the experience of another being. To have empathy, you have to see yourself as that other being. You have to take their experience into yourself and feel/think about their experience from their perspective. Then you have to regain your own perspective and balance it with what you've just learned. It helps if you have to have a solid sense of your own self to return to. Balancing "I" with "we" and "they" is key.

When you see yourself as sacred, you can understand the sacredness of others.

CARRYING AROUND TOXIC ANGER, TOXIC SHAME, AND HATRED IS HARD WORK.

It can interfere with our relationships. It can lead us to self-medicate with alcohol or drugs. Thinking too much about what happened, or who did it, can take time away from the things we want to do in life.

Some survivors of intergenerational trauma say they choose to forgive, so they can stop the pain. Other Indigenous people say forgiveness isn't possible and isn't necessary.

222

"The concept of forgiveness no matter the wrong is a Christian one. The repainting of powerful peoples who fought and died for our land as gentle, passive peoples striving always to be the bigger person is as false as the pope wearing a headdress. We can have dignity without honouring our oppressors. . . . We can be angry without letting that anger consume us. . . . We do not have to forgive."

TARA HOUSKA
(ANISHINAABE)

→ Does forgiveness break the cycle of inter-generational trauma?
→ Is forgiveness possible when wrongs are not made right?
→ Does forgiveness build understanding?
→ Why are victims always given the task of doing the forgiving?
→ How is power part of forgiveness and understanding?

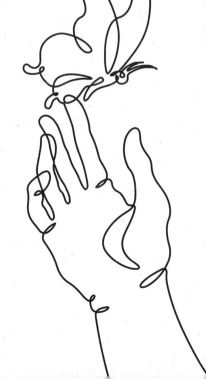

12 PRINCIPLES OF INDIGENOUS PHILOSOPHY

These ideas were gathered at a conference of Indigenous elders, spiritual leaders, and professionals in Lethbridge, Alberta, in December 1982.

Wholeness/holistic thinking. All things are interrelated. Everything in the universe is part of a single whole. Everything is connected in some way to everything else. It is only possible to understand something if we understand how it is connected to everything else.

Change. Everything is in a state of constant change. One season falls upon the other. People are born, live, and die. All things change. There are two kinds of change: the coming together of things, and the coming apart of things. Both kinds of change are necessary and are always connected to each other.

Change occurs in cycles or patterns. They are not random or accidental. If we cannot see how a particular change is connected it usually means that our standpoint is affecting our perception.

The physical world is real. The spiritual world is real. They are two aspects of one reality. There are separate laws that govern each. Breaking of a spiritual principle will affect the physical world and vice versa. A balanced life is one that honours both.

People are physical and spiritual beings.

People can acquire new gifts, but they must struggle to do so. The process of developing new personal qualities may be called "true learning." There are four dimensions of true learning. A person learns in a whole and balanced manner when the mental, spiritual, physical, and emotional dimensions are involved in the process.

Human development. The spiritual dimension of human development has four related capacities:

- the capacity to have and respond to dreams, visions, ideals, spiritual teachings, goals, and theories
- the capacity to accept these as a reflection of our unknown or unrealized potential
- the capacity to express these using symbols in speech, art, or mathematics
- the capacity to use this symbolic expression toward action directed at making the possible a reality

People must actively participate in the development of their own potential. A person must decide to develop their own potential. The path will always be there for those who decide to travel it. Any person who sets out on a journey of self-development will be aided. Guides, teachers, and protectors will assist the traveller. The only source of failure is a person's own failure to follow the teachings.

EACH MORNING, DECIDE HOW YOU WANT TO LIVE THE DAY

Commit to living from your mind, body, and spirit • Don't take on other people's negative energy • Be grateful and aware of all you have, even if you don't have a lot • Connect to the spirit world and the land every day • Tell yourself that your emotions are temporary, and that you're free to move on to healthier ideas, thoughts, and emotions

Indigenous people often speak about doing things in a "good way." This means that others approve of an action and the way you go about that action. It also means that you choose to live the right way and do the right thing because it serves the health of your spirit to do so. Doing something in a good way means you are creating positive energy for yourself and others in thought and action.

Tewa scholar Gregory Cajete says that healthy societies are created from healthy communities made up of self-determining individuals taking responsibility for their actions and respecting all other things in the universe.

"If I sit in the middle of the woods with all this pain, what am I going to do? If I look up, I see the trees, alive and well and beautiful. How did they become like that? They didn't get mad at anybody to be like this. Ask nature to take care of you. Don't be afraid to talk to nature."

ELDER EDDIE PASHAGUMKUM (CREE)

Healing is about feeling at home in your own body/mind/spirit.

Inuit in Nunavut say that before colonization, everyone was busy. Everyone knew their roles. Everyone had a connection to their ancestors and spirit helpers, so they had guidance on their purpose in life (who they were as people and what they could contribute to the community). Today, people have nothing productive to do because they no longer have to hunt, make clothing, or make snow houses to survive. They have lots of ideas/choices but no purpose. Colonialism forces young people to live within values that are not their own.

Inuit youth say they want cross-cultural collaboration on environmental stewardship and the climate crisis. They want to regain control of Inuit political, economic, educational, and belief systems.

Young people want opportunities to be contributing members of their communities, with value and purpose.

"I went back this summer, and I got to change the narrative for myself. When I went back, it was around the time when they were finding the graves at the residential schools, so there were a lot of ceremonies back home for them. So instead of me just showing up, I was actually a part of helping. I was there and I was like, 'How can I help?' I was never that person before. We did a community smudge, and we've never done that before. Like, I drove the truck and the elders did the rest. We literally smudged the entire community. It was new for me."

MONTANA,
age 25, Shoal Lake #40 First
Nation and Peterborough, Ontario

228

There are different cultural protocols/ rituals in different Indigenous nations for expelling negative energy/spirits like the wittigo.

- If you know, or have access to, a medicine person, elder, or knowledge keeper, ask for guidance.
- Ask the staff at your local Friendship Centre, community centre, or health centre if they have cultural advisers or a culture team, and if you can make an appointment.

There are many ways to move/get rid of negative energy:

- ask for help from your ancestors and spirit guides, then pay attention to your dreams and what comes to you in the waking world
- tell the negative energy/spirit to go away ("You are not welcome here. Go away, I want to sleep")
- set a barrier: paint a medicine shield, put sacred medicines around doors/windows or around your bed/room
- attend ceremony or ask a medicine person to doctor you
- keep yourself physically/mentally/spiritually/ emotionally strong (eat well, sleep well, think/ do well)
- get in touch with your fear: figure out what it relates to in your past experiences, and what you need to do to feel safe and protected

Every Indigenous nation has its own values and cultural frameworks. The Great Law of Peace is one Haudenosaunee framework. The Diné speak of the Earth People, the Holy People, and the four directions. The medicine wheel is used by the Nehiyawak.

The medicine wheel helps us learn how to live in a particular place (body, mind, spirit, family, community, land . . .) over time. It teaches us about interrelatedness, balance, change, and connection. The medicine wheel also helps us understand human development. We begin each cycle in the east and end in the north. As we take our journey through life, we gain awareness, understanding, knowledge, and wisdom with each turn around the circle. The centre of the circle represents humanity and the energy of human agency. Imagine yourself standing there, with the circle around you in 3D, and you turning around the circle. The medicine wheel is more than a drawing on a page. It's the universe, with you in the middle, in the sacred spot where movement and change are possible.

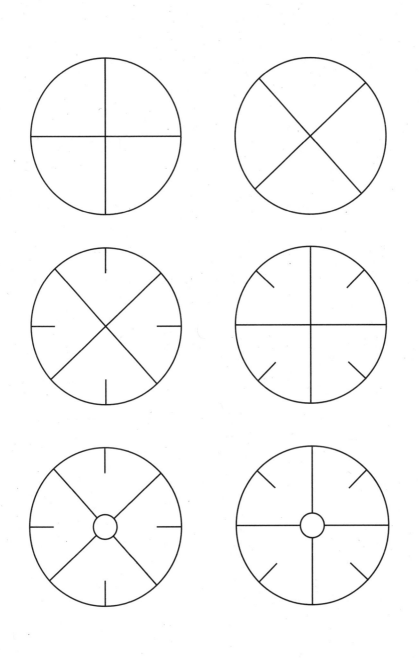

EAST: VISION/SPIRIT

- when we think and have hope
- the guiding vision, seeing what needs to be done
- thinking of ways to create change
- the stories, ceremonies, teachings that bring us awareness and vision

SOUTH: TIME/BODY

- the time it takes to relate to an idea/vision and understand it
- the connections between the land around us and the body we inhabit
- learning about change over time
- learning about relationship

WEST: FEELING/EMOTION

- using the spiritual part of ourselves to gain knowledge
- using reason to figure things out
- using our feelings to know when it's right
- making sense of the world around us

NORTH: MOVEMENT/MIND

- being aware of our behaviour/s
- change comes from action, not just talking and thinking
- a deep understanding of ourselves and the world around us
- new behaviours that embrace change in a conscious way

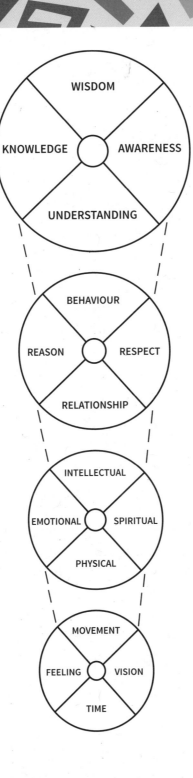

IT'S OKAY . . .

- to talk about feelings
- to ask for help
- to break down
- to cry (especially if you're a boy/man)
- to need support
- to be vulnerable
- to set boundaries
- to go to therapy/counselling/a program
- to not be okay

"I'm finding a voice now, but I didn't always have that. I couldn't heal if I didn't know what was going on. I'm learning the history and about intergenerational trauma. You have to be able to feel all these things before you can work through them. You have to, in order to move forward. If you ignore it, it keeps popping up again and again and again. I'm in a 12-step program, so I feel like it has taught me a lot. I give it a lot of credit, because that's where I found my voice. That's where I learned a whole different way to live, like completely. I'm just starting to share in meetings. It's helpful. That's where I'm learning to find my voice. That's where I kinda learned my coping strategies too. Also therapy, like practicing mindfulness and meditation, and the importance of balancing my thoughts with facts because it is very easy to spiral."

MONTANA,
age 25, Shoal Lake #40 First Nation
and Peterborough, Ontario

Healing is about taking small steps forward, taking a few accidental steps backward, and then trying again. Power comes from our connection to our deepest self, to what is real. We're always beginners.

"Sometimes the hard way is the best way to learn. Going through difficult times in my life really made me the person I am now. It taught me many things."

KENNEDY,
age 16, Flying Post #72 First
Nation and Timmins, Ontario

In 2020, 24-year-old Tristen Durocher walked 635 kilometres (395 miles) from his home in Air Ronge, Saskatchewan, to the legislative building in the provincial capital. He set up a tipi and did a 44-day ceremonial fast to raise awareness about the high number of young Indigenous people who are dying of suicide. He wanted to convince the provincial government to adopt a suicide prevention bill it had recently voted down. The bill has since been adopted.

"It was different at home this last time — because I changed, you know what I mean? Before, I felt like I didn't have anything to offer. I didn't see any hope, I didn't even want to be alive. So I didn't see these events, these ceremonies, any community things, as something even worth going to. I didn't feel a part of it because I was so stuck in my addiction, and my self-centredness. I look forward to going home now."

MONTANA,
age 25, Shoal Lake #40 First Nation and Peterborough, Ontario

IF TRAUMA CAN BE PASSED DOWN, THEN SO CAN HEALING. BE A GOOD ANCESTOR.

To do something in a "good way" in the Indigenous universe is to create beneficial/harmonious energy in thought and action. We each have so much power. Our words and thoughts have power. It's important to be kind and to have self-discipline. We are what we do, think, and say.

Becoming fully human is about risking connection. When we emerge from the spirit world at birth, we need to be surrounded by a strong network of relationships based on the Indigenous 4 Rs (respect, responsibility, reciprocity, relationships). These values teach us the skills we need to know ourselves, know others, and work for the benefit of community. If we do not have that network in childhood, then we have two paths: we can spend a lifetime repeating the disconnection we have inherited, or we can seek change through connection.

YOU ARE A SACRED BEING. YOU HAVE A RIGHT TO BE HERE. DO MORE THAN SURVIVE. THRIVE.

INVOCATION

Read along, out loud:

I am a sovereign being.

I am joined together with all that is.

I ask for balance and harmony within myself and in our world.

I am grateful for the guidance and connection that I receive from the human world, the natural world, and the spirit world.

Please open a path before me and give me an opportunity to bring goodness into the world.

ACKNOWLEDGEMENTS

Big hyi-hyi to Montana, Kelsey, and Kennedy for speaking with me about your life experiences and hopes for the future. This book is better because you are in it. Thank you, Montana, for sharing your poetry. Many thanks to Riel Dupuis-Rossi (Kanien'kehá:ka, Algonquin, Italian), trauma therapist in private practice, and Dr. Jeannine Carriere (Métis), professor of social work at the University of Victoria, for doing expert reads and providing comments and feedback on the manuscript. You challenged me to go deeper, and the book is better for your care and input.

RESOURCES

We Matter Toolkit for Indigenous Youth
Toolkit activities and videos to watch on your own, with a friend, or a family member

https://wemattercampaign.org/toolkits/youth

We Matter Toolkit for Support Workers
Be your own advocate! Ask your teachers, caseworker, counsellor, or other adult helpers to watch these videos and complete these activities

https://wemattercampaign.org/toolkits/support-workers

Healing with the Seven Sacred Teachings
Free, downloadable, dual-language (Mi'kmaw/ English) colouring book for all ages, based on Indigenous cultural values

https://www.mcgill.ca/morethanwords/files/morethanwords/
healing_with_the_seven_sacred_teachings_colouring_book.pdf

Native Youth Sexual Health Network
Resources/toolkits/workshops on Two-Spirit mental health, Indigenized harm reduction, sexual health, and environmental violence and reproductive justice, by and for Indigenous youth in the US and Canada

https://www.nativeyouthsexualhealth.com/

We R Native

Info on culture, life, relationships, mental health, and community service for Indigenous youth in the US, with an "Ask Auntie/Uncle" Q&A service

https://www.wernative.org/

Finding Our Power Together

Online programs for youth, one-on-one mentorship, and Young Leaders Circle

https://findingourpowertogether.com/

National Indian Residential Schools Crisis Line

24/7 crisis services and emotional support for Indigenous people in Canada: 1-800-721-0066

https://www.irsss.ca/

Hope for Wellness Helpline

24/7 mental health counselling, crisis intervention, and resources for Indigenous peoples across Canada in English and French (phone/chat), as well as Ojibway, Cree, and Inuktitut (phone)

1-855-242-3310 or chat: https://www.hopeforwellness.ca/

HeretoHelp — Indigenous

Information on mental health and substance use

https://www.heretohelp.bc.ca/indigenous

MindShift

App from Anxiety Canada with tools to deal with worry, panic, perfectionism, social anxiety, and phobias. The Community Forum helps you find/offer peer-to-peer support

https://www.anxietycanada.com/resources/mindshift-cbt/

Ditch the Label
Info for people aged 12–25 on mental health, bullying, identity, and relationships, with an online community forum

https://www.ditchthelabel.org/

Kids Help Phone
Learn about mental health, build your skills, connect with other young people, work with a counsellor, and get crisis support 24/7 across Canada

1-800-668-6868; text 686868
https://kidshelpphone.ca/

Suicide Prevention Lifeline
24/7 support for Indigenous people in the US

1-800-273-TALK (8255)
https://suicidepreventionlifeline.org/help-yourself/
native-americans/

Strong Hearts Native Helpline
24/7 domestic violence and dating violence helpline for Native Americans and Alaska Natives in the US, offering culturally appropriate support and advocacy
1-844-7NATIVE (762-8483)

Chat: https://strongheartshelpline.org/

National Indigenous Women's Resource Center

Advocacy and national leadership to end violence against American Indian, Alaska Native, and Native Hawaiian women in the US

406-477-3896
info@niwrc.org
https://www.niwrc.org/

National Native American Boarding School Healing Coalition

Education and advocacy for boarding school survivors and descendants in the US, resources for self-care and trauma, and curriculum for teachers

612-354-7700
https://boardingschoolhealing.org/

Center for Native American Youth

National education and advocacy organization that works alongside Native youth (ages 24 and under) on reservations, in rural villages, and in urban spaces across the US to improve health, safety, and well-being

https://www.cnay.org/

National Inuit Youth Council

Guidance and input for Inuit youth in Canada
https://www.itk.ca/niyc/

United National Indian Tribal Youth (UNITY)

Webinars and an annual youth-led conference focusing on the spiritual, mental, physical, and social development of Indigenous youth in the US

https://unityinc.org/

Assembly of Seven Generations

Land-based learning, weekly youth gatherings, Young Men's Support Circle, Indigenous language drop-ins, webinars, and videos

https://www.a7g.ca/

Indian Youth of America

Inter-tribal summer youth camps for Indigenous youth ages 10–14 in the US

https://indianyouthofamerica.org/

Canadian Roots Exchange

Youth-led projects, youth policy school, research hub, peer program, healing programs, and a justice program for Indigenous youth, plus national gatherings to build dialogue between Indigenous and non-Indigenous youth in Canada

https://canadianroots.ca/

Right To Play

Community-led, culturally relevant play-based programs that build life skills for Indigenous youth in Canada

https://righttoplay.com/en-ca/national-offices/
national-office-canada/get-involved/indigenous-programs/

Youth in Care Canada

Research, policy development, advocacy, training for social service providers, post-secondary scholarships for youth currently/formerly in foster care, and a list of local/regional/provincial youth in care networks and groups

1-800-790-7074
info@youthincare.ca
https://youthincare.ca/

Indspire

Bursaries and scholarships for Indigenous students in Canada

https://indspire.ca/

The American Indian College Fund

Webinars, videos, and financial support for Native American students in the US

https://collegefund.org/#n

The Legacy Project

Resources and information on intergenerational trauma and trauma-informed practice

https://www.traumastoryhealing.ca/

Indigenous content creators

#IndigenousTikTok   #NativeTumblr
#NativeTikTok   #IndigenousInstagram
#IndigenousTumblr   #NativeInstagram

CITATIONS & PERMISSIONS

Page xii: "Flashback Protocol" adapted from Kent Smith (2009) and Babette Rothchild (2001).

Page 4: 60 million acres: Indian Land Tenure Foundation via https://iltf.org/land-issues/issues/.

Page 5–6: Text for "Intergenerational Impacts" adapted from the Aboriginal Healing Foundation Program Handbook, second edition (Ottawa, 1999).

Page 8–9: Lyrics to "Why Us" courtesy of N'we Jinan Artists and inPath.

Page 10: Natasha Reimer-Okemow quotation: CBC News via https://www.cbc.ca/news/canada/manitoba/cfs-child-family-services-residential-schools-1.6069510.

Page 16: Maria Yellowhorse Brave Heart, "From Intergenerational Trauma to Intergenerational Healing," keynote address at the Wellbreity Conference, Denver, Colorado, 2005.

Page 19–21: ACE questionnaire: Felitti et al., Centers for Disease Control and Prevention and Kaiser Permanente, 1998.

Page 24: Kateri-Akiwenzie-Damm quotation: Editors Toronto Blog via https://editorstorontoblog.com/2022/08/04/editor-for-life-kateri-akiwenzie-damm-publisher-and-managing-editor-at-kegedonce-press-writer-and-professor/.

Page 31: Bloody Island Massacre, 1850: "A History of American Indians in California: Historic Sites," National Parks Service via https://www.nps.gov/parkhistory/online _books/5views/5views1h8.htm and *Native American History: A Chronology of a Culture's Vast Achievements and Their Links to World Events*, Judith E. Nies, Random House (1996).

Page 31: Battleford, 1885: "Public Hanging Led to Years of Repression," Doug Cuthand, *Saskatoon Star-Phoenix*, Dec. 1, 2018, via https://thestarphoenix .com/opinion/columnists/cuthand-public-hanging-led -to-years-of-repression-for-first-nations and "Battleford Industrial Residential School," *Shattering the Silence: The Hidden History of Indian Residential Schools in Saskatchewan*, Shuana Niessen, Faculty of Education, University of Regina (2017), via https://www2.uregina .ca/education/saskindianresidentialschools/battleford -industrial-residential-school/.

Page 32: The Pas, 1971: "The Death of Helen Betty Osborne," The Aboriginal Justice Implementation Commission (1999), via http://www.ajic.mb.ca/volumell /chapter1.html.

Page 32: Morice River, 2019–Present: All Out for Wedzin Kwa, Gidimt'en Checkpoint, via https://www.yintahaccess .com/ and Unist'ot'en: Heal the People, Heal the Land via http://unistoten.camp/.

Page 35: School suspension rates: "The Toronto District School Board's Student Group Overviews," TDSB Research and Information Services (2015).

Page 38: "Reverse Poem," "Untitled," and "Teach Me My History," courtesy of Montana Paypompee.

Page 39: Wilfred Peltier quotation: *Aboriginal Beliefs, Values, and Aspirations*, Pearson Canada (2011).

Page 42: Eric Shirt quotation: Facebook.

Page 43: @kawisahawii post: Facebook.

Page 44: Population stats: "Most Native Americans Live in Cities, Not Reservations," Joe Whittle, *The Guardian*, Sept. 4, 2017, via https://www.theguardian.com/us -news/2017/sep/04/native-americans-stories-california; Urban Indian Health Institute via https://www.uihi.org /urban-indian-health/; "Urbanization and Indigenous Peoples in Canada," National Association of Friendship Centres via https://nafc.ca/downloads/un-questionnaire -from-the-special-rapporteur-on-the-rights-of-indigenous -peoples-2021.pdf; "Housing, Income, and Residential Dissimilarity Among Indigenous People in Canadian Cities," Thomas Anderson, Statistics Canada, via https://www150.statcan.gc.ca/n1/pub/75-006-x/2019001 /article/00018-eng.htm.

Page 60: "Urban Land-Based Healing: A Northern Intervention Strategy," Nicole Redvers, Melanie Nadeau, Donald Prince, *International Journal of Indigenous Health*, Vol. 16 Issue 2, 2021.

Page 72: What is Harm Reduction?, Fraser Health, via https://www.fraserhealth.ca/health-topics-a-to-z/mental -health-and-substance-use/harm-reduction/what-is-harm -reduction#.Y3wiYrLMITA.

Page 78, Page 109, and Page 194: Screenshots: "Lateral Violence a 'Colonial Hangover' We Need to Heal: Prof," Aboriginal Peoples Television Network, via https://www .aptnnews.ca/infocus/lateral-violence-a-colonial-hangover -we-need-to-heal-prof/.

Page 79–81: Susan Aglukark screenshot and post comments: Facebook.

Page 88: Rod Jeffries, conference presentation to the Assembly of Manitoba Chiefs, via YouTube.

Page 90: Ilirasuk definition: Susan Aglukark website blog, via http://susanaglukark.com/.

Page 92: Youth suicides: "The Office of the Chief Coroner's Death Review of the Youth Suicides at the Pikangikum First Nation 2006–2008," Dr. Andrew McCallum (2012).

Page 95: Maria Campbell quotation: "Métis Women's Strength-Based Kindness Toolkit," Les Femmes Michif Otipemisiwak, no date, via https://www.mnbc.ca/wp -content/uploads/2020/06/strength_based_lateral _kindness_toolkit.pdf.

Page 97: Isaac Chamakese quotation: "Wahkohtowin: Cree Natural Law," BearPaw Media and Education, via https://www.youtube.com/watch?v=NTXMrn2BZB0.

Page 100: Tasha Beeds quotation: "Lateral Violence a 'Colonial Hangover' We Need to Heal: Prof," Aboriginal Peoples Television Network, via https://www.aptnnews.ca /infocus/lateral-violence-a-colonial-hangover-we-need-to -heal-prof/.

Page 102: Fred Campiou quotation: "Are We Seeking Pimatisiwin or Creating Pomewin? Implications for Water Policy," LaBoucane-Benson et al., *The International Indigenous Policy Journal* 3(3), 2021.

Page 103: Patti LaBoucane-Benson: "Moving Beyond Lateral Violence," presentation at the Growing Our

Relations: Wahkohtowin conference, North Central Alberta Child and Family Services, 2013.

Page 121: "Are They Really Your Friend? 15 Signs That Suggest Otherwise," Ditch the Label, https://www.ditch thelabel.org/are-they-really-your-friend-15-signs-that -suggest-otherwise/.

Page 123: Adapted from "How Do You See Your Relationships with Other People?," Key Learnings from the Application of the Aboriginal-Informed Growth and Empowerment Measure, Melissa Haswell et al., School of Public Health and Social Work, Queensland University of Technology, via https://www.nhmrc.gov.au /sites/default/files/documents/attachments/symposium /melissa_haswell.pdf.

Page 135: Sex as Abuse vs. Sex as Positive Energy, adapted from "How Sexual Abuse Can Shape Understandings of Sex," Living Well, https://livingwell.org.au/relationships /partners-sexual-intimacy/.

Page 137: Adapted from "Healthy Relationships," Jen Moff, via https://thejenmoff.com/.

Page 147: Funding for health services: "Side Conversations Root of First Nations Health Tragedy," Dr. Alika Lafontaine, CBC News, April 26, 2017, via https://www.cbc.ca/news/canada/saskatchewan /first-nations-health-tragedy-1.4082876.

Page 151: "ADHD Characteristics in Canadian Aboriginal Children," Lola Baydala et al., *Journal of Attention Disorders,* 9(4), 2006.

Page 152: Pueblo Food Experience Project: "Blue Corn and Melons: Meet the Seed Keepers

Reviving Ancient, Resilient Crops," Samuel Gilbert, *The Guardian*, Apr. 18, 2022, via https://www.theguardian.com/environment/2022/apr/18/seed-keeper-indigenous-farming-acoma.

Page 156–157: Western medicine does not understand Indigenous medicine: "Creating Space for Indigenous Healing Practices in Patient Care Plans," Lindsey Logan et al., *Canadian Medical Education Journal* (2020).

Page 158: Two-Spirit: Trans Care BC, Provincial Health Services Authority, via http://www.phsa.ca/transcarebc/gender-basics-education/terms-concepts/two-spirit.

Page 158: Goneness: "Blood Borders," *Indian Country: Essays on Contemporary Native Culture*, Gail Guthrie Valaskakis, Wilfred Laurier University Press (2005).

Page 159: N. Scott Momaday quotation: *The Names: A Memoir*, N. Scott Momaday, University of Arizona Press (1987).

Page 162: 5-4-3-2-1 exercise adapted from Alexander Lowen.

Page 164–165: HALT exercise adapted from 12-step principles.

Page 166: Gabor Maté quotation: *When the Body Says No: The Cost of Hidden Stress*, Gabor Maté, Penguin Random House (2004).

Page 174: Bongiwe Maome and Hannah Battiste quotations: Networks for Change project, *Circle Back: Stories of Reflection, Connection, and Transformation*, Claudia Mitchell, Participatory Culture Lab, McGill University (2021).

Page 174: Cy Standing quotation: Facebook.

Page 186: Deion Pearce and Minnie Akeeagok quotations: "Iqaluit Teens Take to the Street to Demand More Suicide Prevention for Nunavummiut," CBC News, via https://www.cbc.ca/news/canada/north/iqaluit-suicide-prevention-students-youth-nunavut-1.6252374.

Page 194: Joe Couture: "In Memoriam — Dr. Joseph Couture," Marilyn Buffalo, July 11, 2007.

Page 195: "Reclaiming Nehiyaw Governance in the Territory of Maskwacis through Wahkohtowin (Kinship)," Paulina R. Johnson, University of Western Ontario, 2017.

Page 196: Tamara Joseph quotation: "Elsipogtog Youth Group Aims to Develop Future Community Leaders," Oscar Baker III, CBC News, via https://www.cbc.ca/news/indigenous/elsipogtog-first-nation-youth-leadership-1.6328852.

Page 197: Hope for Healing: "Cousins on Alberta First Nation Say Garbage Just the Start of Path to Rebuild Community Spirit," Colleen Underwood, CBC News, via https://www.cbc.ca/news/canada/calgary/hope-for-healing-1.6062442.

Page 198: Ocean Pottle-Shiwak quotation: "Inuk Woman Creates Language Book to Showcase Fading Inuktitut Dialect," Heidi Atter, CBC News, via https://www.cbc.ca/news/canada/newfoundland-labrador/inuk-woman-dialect-book-1.6208188.

Page 202: Tr'ondëk Hwëch'in Teaching and Working Farm: "1st Crop of Young First Nation Farmers Graduates in Dawson City," Cheryl Kawaja, CBC News, via https://www.cbc.ca/news/canada/north/farm-school

-tr-ondek-hwech-in-first-nation-graduates-1.3754007.

Page 204: Sustainable development: Indigenous-Led Clean Energy Project Map, via https://indigenouscleanenergy.com/connect-learn /indigenous-led-clean-energy-project-map/ and "Developing Clean Energy Projects on Tribal Lands," US Department of Energy, via https://www.nrel.gov/docs /fy13osti/57748.pdf.

Page 205: Population stats: National Congress of American Indians, via https://www.ncai.org/about-tribes /demographics and "Indigenous Youth in Canada," Statistics Canada, via https://www150.statcan.gc.ca/n1 /pub/42-28-0001/2021001/article/00004-eng.htm.

Page 208: Community Mobilization Hub: "The Prince Albert Hub and the Emergence of Collaborative Risk-Driven Community Safety," Dale R. McFee et al., Canadian Police College Discussion Paper (2014).

Page 208: Prince Albert Police Association quotation: "New Details Emerge in Homicide of Saskatchewan 13-Month-Old Tanner Brass," Yasmine Ghania, CBC News, via https://www.cbc.ca/news/canada/saskatoon /baby-tanner-new-details-emerge-1.6484733.

Page 213: Jeff Thomas quotation: Where Are the Children?, Legacy of Hope, via https://legacyofhope.ca /portfolio-items/wherearethechildren/?portfolioCats=35.

Page 213: Michael Thrasher: "Winds of Change: The Medicine Wheel as Movement," presentation at the Celebrating Indigenous Knowledges: Peoples, Lands, and Cultures conference, Department of Indigenous Studies, Trent University, 2010.

Page 223: Tara Zhaabowekwe Houska quotation: Facebook.

Page 226: Gregory Cajete: "Rebuilding Sustainable Indigenous Communities," presentation at the Celebrating Indigenous Knowledges: Peoples, Lands, and Cultures conference, Department of Indigenous Studies, Trent University, 2010.

Page 227: Eddie Pashagumkum quotation: "Land, Life, and Knowledge in Chisasibi: Intergenerational Healing in the Bush," Ioana Radu et al., *Decolonization: Indigeneity, Education & Society* (3), 2014.

Page 227: Inuit youth: National Inuit Climate Change Strategy, Inuit Tapiriit Kanatami, via https://www.itk.ca/wp-content/uploads/2019/06/ITK_Climate-Change -Strategy_English_lowres.pdf.

Quotations from Montana: personal communication, November 6, 2021.

Quotations from Kelsey: personal communication, November 12, 2021.

Quotations from Kennedy: personal communication, December 12, 2021.

This book is also available as a Global Certified Accessible™ (GCA) ebook. ECW Press's ebooks are screen reader friendly and are built to meet the needs of those who are unable to read standard print due to blindness, low vision, dyslexia or a physical disability.

At ECW Press, we want you to enjoy our books in whatever format you like. If you've bought a print copy, just send an email to ebook@ecwpress.com and include:

- the book title
- the name of the store where you purchased it
- a screenshot or picture of your order/receipt number and your name
- your preference of file type: PDF (for desktop reading), ePub (for a phone/tablet, Kobo, or Nook), mobi (for Kindle)

A real person will respond to your email with your ebook attached. Please note this offer is only for copies bought for personal use and does not apply to school or library copies.

Thank you for supporting an independently owned Canadian publisher with your purchase!

This book is made of paper from well-managed FSC® - certified forests, recycled materials, and other controlled sources.